The Human Right to Water in Latin America

International Water Law

Volumes published in this Brill Research Perspectives title are listed at *brill.com/rpwl*

The Human Right to Water in Latin America

Challenges to Implementation and Contribution to the Concept

By

Anna Berti Suman

BRILL

LEIDEN | BOSTON

This paperback book edition is simultaneously published as issue 3.2 (2018) of *International Water Law*, DOI 10.1163/23529369-12340010.

Library of Congress Control Number: 2018937573

Typeface for the Latin, Greek, and Cyrillic scripts: "Brill". See and download: brill.com/brill-typeface.

ISBN 978-90-04-36780-7 (paperback)
ISBN 978-90-04-36781-4 (e-book)

This book is printed on acid-free paper and produced in a sustainable manner.

To Tina, mentor and friend

Contents

Acknowledgements

First and foremost, I would like to extend my sincere gratitude to Dr. Salman Mohamed Ahmed Salman, Editor-in-Chief of this series, for his advice and guidance. Moreover, I would like to acknowledge my appreciation for the thorough comments of the Reviewer and the Editorial Board of this series for their constructive input. My deepest thanks go to my advisors at the University of Bologna, Professor Susanna Mancini and Professor Francesco Biagi, whose wise counsel and insightful commentaries have made this work possible. I would also like to acknowledge my indebtedness to my supervisor at the *Fundación Chile*, Professor Axel Dourojeanni Ricordi, for initiating me to the science of water systems engineering and watershed management. My gratitude goes to Dr. Agustina Mohando, expert of the *Fundación Chile*, for her invaluable support and her enthusiastic encouragement. Special thanks to Professor David Altman of the Pontifical Catholic University of Chile for his constructive criticism and suggestions. I am also very grateful to Professor Thierry Tanquerel and Dr. Zohra Kibboua for their advice and for the knowledge I gained during their seminars at the University of Geneva.

List of Abbreviations

ACUMAR	*Autoridad de la Cuenca Matanza-Riachuelo*
EU	European Union
IWRM	Integrated Water Resource Management
LA	Latin America
MS	Market Service
PbWM	Public Water Management
PS	Public Service
PvWM	Private Water Management
RtW	Right to Water
SA	*SuizAgua*
UN	United Nations
WB	World Bank
WRs	Water Rights

The Human Right to Water in Latin America

Challenges to Implementation and Contribution to the Concept

Anna Berti Suman
Tilburg Institute for Law, Technology and Society (TILT), Tilburg Law School, Tilburg University, The Netherlands
a.bertisuman@uvt.nl

Abstract

This monograph investigates the development of the right to water (RtW) and of water law in the Latin American context. Specifically, it examines the significance of Latin American (LA) constitutional evolution, doctrine, and jurisprudential contribution in stimulating the social, political, and economic debate on the RtW, regionally and worldwide. Firstly, an overview on the RtW in LA constitutions is provided and the impact of the findings is highlighted. The main LA water management systems are then reviewed with an acknowledgment that an analysis of the RtW has to take account of its application in specific contexts. The intrinsic connection between the RtW and the role of the private sector is examined through specific insights into the highly privatized Chilean water services. Lessons learnt from the LA experience are outlined in the conclusion and their relevance for the global debate on the RtW is illustrated.

Keywords

Constitutional Law – International Law – Latin America – privatization – right to water – water law

Introduction

I *The Monograph's Structure and Goals*

The right to water (RtW) is nowadays a central issue in the social, political, and economic debate worldwide. A large and heterogeneous number of solutions

 | DOI 10.1163/9789004367814_002

have been proposed with the aim of establishing a balance among the interests of civic society, those of the private sector, respect for the environment, and public finance concerns. The main aim of this monograph is to illustrate and analyze lessons from Latin America, contributing to the international debate on the governance of the RtW. This analysis is performed by questioning the role that each stakeholder should have in the debate with a view to discussing best practices to harmonize the RtW with the interests of the concerned stakeholders.

This introduction sets the scene for the relevance of transboundary water issues, the dual nature of water and its economic value, through the analysis of the debate ongoing at the international level. The following sections depart from this supranational perspective to delve into local scenarios, where the RtW is transposed in the domestic constitutional laws of Latin American (LA) countries and is examined through its interplay with water management systems.

Part A investigates the broader, specifically Latin American, discussion on the responsibility of the state towards the right to water, when it is recognized in constitutions and when it is acknowledged through different legal tools. It is argued that the state has the obligation to ensure the RtW regardless of the payment capacity of its citizens. It is investigated whether the state has a duty to grant a quantitative and qualitative minimum of fresh water to everyone through subsidies, even if this impinges on private enterprise interests. The consequences of a state's decision-making process that does not take into account the RtW are illustrated through the case studies of Cochabamba, Bolivia, and Mendoza, Argentina.

The examples presented in Part A serve as an illustration of the limits of the law in resolving water management issues on the basis of the lessons learnt from Latin America. It is argued that countries with a very different legal scenario on water face similar issues, whereas countries presenting a similar water regulation regime may substantially diverge on water matters. This circumstance shows that the legal scenario does not always match the reality, which is a lesson interesting not only to Latin America but also the broader international community. The ultimate aim of this discussion is to define the appropriate role for the legislative branch in the debate on water policies. Furthermore, the judicial system is examined under the analytical lens of its suitability to settle water disputes. Overall, the need to focus the debate on specific issues rather than on general statements is stressed.

The linking element that bridges the transition from Part A to Part B is the discussion of the fundamental question on whether the right to water as a human right is in antithesis with privatization (Part A, Section IV). The question is answered by the argument that, in principle, the recognition of water as a human right does not prevent the possibility of privatizing the service, as long as the state monitors the private provider's operations and complies with its obligations to ensure the RtW.

The imperative to always consider the RtW 'in context', beyond its abstract recognition in the constitution, leads to a focus on the main LA water management systems. In light of the need to apply the RtW to existing water management frameworks, in Part B the different models for water service management in Latin America are analyzed. Additionally, the dominant LA models are compared with the European Union (EU) legal framework. This way the assumption that the recognition of water as a human right does not *a priori* prevent the possibility to privatize the service is tested. The analysis of the debate between private and public water management and the consideration of each model's advantages and disadvantages show that the choice of the private or the public provider should not be a definitive solution. Arguably, a compromise between the two models, such as a public-private partnership, may prove to be the best option. The urgency of appropriate solutions for water governance demands a more technical approach based on the specificities of each river basin unit is stressed and is a lesson applicable to different water management models, regardless of their private or public nature.

The notion that the private sector is responsible of RtW violations often suggests the need to focus on the controversial relationship between the RtW and the private sector. Consequently, a specific insight into the relationship between the market and the RtW is presented in Part C. In this Part, the particularities of Chile's highly privatized water framework are described in order to pinpoint the connection between the political history of the country and its regulation of water services. The aim of these reflections is to contend that, in spite of the partial or total privatization of the water service, the state should have control over the provider in order to secure the RtW. Moreover, the Chilean case, with its dominant role of the private water market, offers an opportunity to reflect not only on the importance of the engagement of all the affected stakeholders in the debate on water, but also on the compelling need for a wise compromise among them.

In the Conclusion, the lessons learnt from discussion throughout this monograph are summarized and confronted. The reflections on the limits of the law in resolving water management issues and the widespread independency of water issues from the legal framework adopted is outlined with a view to asserting the mismatch between the legal data and the reality of water challenges and conflicts. The analysis of the role of the legislative branch and of the judiciary, in the debate on water policies brings forward the controversy on the choice of the 'most suitable' water management model. Beyond the differences of each context, the general need for a focus on the specificities of each river basin unit is reaffirmed. The final message derived from the reflections developed throughout this monograph is that the recognition of water as a human right does not prevent the possibility of privatizing the service, provided that the obligations of the state towards the right to water are fulfilled. Ultimately, the key role of the engagement of all the affected stakeholders in the debate on water is stressed, with a view to achieving a constructive and open-minded compromise for jointly facing current water challenges.

II *The Dual Nature of Water*

Water is an indispensable source of life, but at the same time it is an economic good. Affirming that water has a 'double nature' means considering the multiple components of this resource. However, 'dual' may be a too limited word to describe the potential 'natures' of water. Nevertheless, two basic components of the resource can be pinpointed. As Salman and McInerney-Lankford illustrate, defining the human right to water is a complex task due to the fact that "water is both a vital and a minimum need, and therefore indispensable to human life. Denying people water is to deny them the right to life."[1] However, water is not only seen as "a social good and a human need, but also as a commodity, the economic value of which must be recognized." This dual nature is underlined in the Chilean Water Law, as it will be examined further in Part C below. As a matter of fact, in Chile two texts provide for the rights of private citizens over water (granted by the 1980 Constitution[2] and the 1981 Water Code)[3] and for water as a national property for public use (as stated by the 1981 Water Code; the Constitution lacks a similar provision).

The uses that fall under the first 'nature of water' division are, first of all, the human consumption of drinkable water and the use of water for sanitation; secondly, water used for agriculture (and, therefore, to produce human sustenance); and thirdly, water as an essential element of the ecosystem (therefore, of life itself).[4] The uses that can be identified under the second division, the economic component, are those associated with industry, the mining sector, and power generation. Furthermore, the economic nature of water must be

1 S. M. A. Salman & S. McInerney-Lankford, *The Human Right to Water: Legal and Policy Dimensions* (Washington, D.C.: The World Bank, 2004) at 3.

2 Constitución Política de la República de Chile, 1980, art. 19(24).

3 Codigo de Aguas, Decreto con Fuerza de Ley 1122, 29 August 1981.

4 C. R. Sáez-Muñoz, '*Privatized Water Rights and Services in Chile 1981–2011: Flowing Towards the Mainstream?*' (Ph.D. Thesis no. 1035, Graduate Institute, Genenva, 2014), at 36–40.

considered in combination with a further element, which seems to identify the point where the first division encounters the second, namely, that water becomes an economic good also when it is 'sold' to users by those enterprises charged with its management (whether public or private).

Although present throughout the whole monograph, the economic dimension of RtW in its interplay with the market and the private sector is stressed in Part B when dealing with privatized models of water management and in Part C when analyzing the Chilean water framework. Yet both Parts find their basis in Part A, which addresses the key question of whether the privatization of the water service is in conflict with the right to water.

The economic value of water was enshrined in the Dublin Statement on Water and Sustainable Development 1992 (Dublin Declaration),[5] issued in the context of an international conference organized in Dublin under the auspices of the United Nations (UN). The evidence of the dual and somehow contradictory nature of the water resource is underlined through an analysis of the Principles. Indeed, water is defined as essential to life and for the environment. Principle 2 requires the participation of users, technicians and politicians in its management. Moreover, the central role of women in procurement, management and protection of water is also affirmed (Principle 3). Notwithstanding these imperatives, just few lines below the Declaration defines water as an economic good in each of its phases.

The context under which the Declaration was adopted is relevant. At that time, the International Monetary Fund and the World Bank were encouraging states to privatize water services and were providing substantially financing for projects leading to water privatization. In the same period, a widespread wave of privatization was taking place, from the generalized privatization led by Prime Minister Margaret Thatcher in Great Britain, to the sale of the water and sanitation services of Buenos Aires, Argentina.

The Dublin Declaration affirms that free water would have led to a squandering of it, while reflecting on its cost makes citizens more responsible for its wise and sustainable use. The idea was that a water service financed by users, and not by public funds, would reduce the squandering of water.[6]

A realistic debate on water cannot disregard the economic value of water resources and cannot fossilize itself on abstract statements on the inviolable nature of water, indispensable for life and therefore alien to every type of subordination to private interests. Several international declarations, along

5 Adopted 31 January 1992, Dublin, Ireland, International Confernence on Water and the Enviroment, text available at http://www.un-documents.net/h2o-dub.htm.

6 A-C. Sjölander Holland, *Il Business dell'Acqua* (Milan: Editorale Jaka Book SpA, 2006), at 26.

with a very copious doctrine on the theme, affirm that, in the *summa divisio* of public-private goods, water has to be considered among public goods for its very special characteristics, in order to grant the resource the guarantees linked to that recognition.

The debate on water as a public good has often been built on the dichotomy of water as a public good versus water as a commodity. Nevertheless, this monograph challenges the rhetoric discussion, and advocates for the 'public nature' of the resource. Contrarily, a more appropriate term, 'common-pool resource', is suggested. This distinction derives from the understanding this researcher has of the concept of 'public good' as being a good from which no one can be excluded access, but also as a non-rivalrous resource in the sense that use by one individual does not reduce its availability to others. If it true that every individual should have access to water, clearly water cannot be considered a non-rivalrous good, as abusive use by an individual leads to a reduction in its availability for others.

What is suggested here is the adoption of Ostrom's formula of 'common-pool resource' and the replacing of the dichotomy between public and private good with common and private good. The notion of common-pool resource seems particularly timely to the water debate as it regards water as a good, whose use, in principle, can be denied to potential beneficiaries, and as a resource which, unlike pure public goods, faces problems of overuse, which may diminish its availability for others.[7] The message this monograph wants to bring forward is that water should be managed rationally, and its use should be driven by considerations of fairness and justice, but also by considerations of efficient and sustainable use.

Moreover, the debate on water as a public good often does not take into account that even publicly provided water has a cost and is sold by enterprises that, although publicly owned, should at least recover the cost of the supply, otherwise the service will become a burden on public finances. Water has a cost for the provider, and for this reason the cost for the user should not be called into question. The central point here is to decide the fairness of the

---

7 E. Ostrom, *Governing the Commons: The Evolution of Institutions for Collective Action* (Cambridge: Cambridge University Press, 1990); Statement of Alejandro Vergara Blanco, VII Jornadas de Derecho ambiental, 15 October 2014, Santiago de Chile, Chile; see also I. E. Kornfeld, 'Water: A Public Good or a Commodity?' *in Proceedings of the Annual Meeting of the American Society of International Law, Confronting Complexity*, Vol. 106 (Cambridge: Cambridge University Press, 2012), pp. 49–52; J. M. Buchanan, 'Public Goods in Theory and Practice: A Note on the Minasian-Samuelson Discussion', *Journal of Law and Economics*, Vol. 10 (1967), pp. 193–197.

circumstance that the provider can generate a profit, additional to the recovery of costs, while balancing this profit with the very nature of water as an indispensable, yet limited, resource. As underlined by Salman and McInerney-Lankford, 'the right to water does not necessarily mean that water should be provided free of charge.'[8] However, it should be 'affordable.' The authors wisely point out that 'the Dublin Principles do not explain the concept of "affordability," nor do they suggest means through which its content and meaning could be determined.'[9]

Water is not only a resource but also an element of the nature. From this perspective, this implies that it cannot be considered detached from the environment where it is located. Water management measures must take into account the various stakeholders involved in the area and the area itself with its geological and hydrological features. In the dialogue among the different groups of interests, mainly those supporting environmental concerns and those promoting economic growth, a solution cannot be found that excludes one or the other from the debate: it is neither democratic nor, in the end, the most efficient solution. A balance, a compromise, should inspire our reflections and proposals. A concept that should guide such discussions is that of 'economic sustainability'.[10] Civil society needs to improve its economic potential without being blind to the water crisis that the world is facing. Future generations would demand that the current generation rationalizes its water use while enhancing the economy and achieving profits.

These guidelines clearly emerge from a speech by Mr. Kofi Annan at the 14th Delhi Sustainable Development Summit.[11] Mr. Annan recognized the fundamental relevance of economics: 'Making the transition from the brown to the green economy', he said, 'is perhaps the biggest challenge of our age. It will require leadership, courage and commitment from all the sectors represented here—government, business, academia and civil society.' He mentioned 'sustainability' as being 'at the heart of the global development framework which succeeds the Millennium Development Goals in 2015.' He spoke in realistic terms: 'The private sector is the main engine of the global economy and accounts for two-thirds of the use of natural resources. It has an enormous

---

8 Salman & McInerney-Lankford, supra note 1, at 9.

9 Ibid., at 9.

10 A. Dourojeanni, *Los retos que impone la gestión del agua a la sustentabilidad empresarial*, Documento de divulgación de Acción RSE (Santiago de Chile: Fundación Chile, 2014a), at 2.

11 K. Annan, Keynote Address to the 14th Delhi Sustainable Development Summit, 'Attaining Energy, Water and Food Security for All', 6 February 2014, New Delhi, India.

responsibility, and an indispensable role to play. They can drive research, innovation and investment to facilitate the transition to a green economy.' Mr. Annan added that 'Civil society must also bring their expertise to bear. By working closely with local communities, they are ideally placed to ensure that government policies meet local needs and priorities.' This monograph aims to build on these inspiring statements by discussing the role of the public sector, civil society, the constitution (Part A), and of the private sector and market models (Parts B and C) in the achievement of best practices in water governance in accordance with the human right to water.

III *The Transboundary Approach to Water Issues*

The current scarcity of natural resources and, in particular, the water crisis is recognized worldwide. While some sources are somehow 'linked' to a country because they are inherent to its land (for example, coal), water resources are often shared by multiple countries, through rivers, lakes and rainfall. Thus pollution of a water source is necessarily a 'shared concern' and requires an approach that goes beyond national borders. Water is a shared resource and therefore a transboundary approach is needed to deal the current water crisis.

Public interest towards water protection has led to various forms of cooperation and association among the global community. For example, the World Water Council, located in Marseille, France, organizes the Mundial Water Forum every three years, and the Global Water Partnership seeks to advance governance and management of water resources through a series of initiatives, among which the launch of the Global Water Partnership Strategy Towards 2020.[12] These two organizations are closely linked to the World Bank, and the economic component plays a fundamental role within them. In 2001, they jointly launched the Camdessus Panel report 'Financing Water for All'[13] at the third Mundial Water Forum in Kyoto, Japan. The Report called for an increase in the annual investment in water services from US$75 million to US$180 million. Furthermore, the Report set out the goal of achieving full cost recovery for water projects, stressing the importance of the engagement of private enterprises in the water sector and reflecting on how to reduce the risks for those companies investing in the sector. Members of the Panel included

12 Sjölander Holland, supra note 6, at 123–125.

13 J. Winpenny, *Financing Water for All*, Report of the World Panel on Financing Water Infrastructure, Chair, Michel Camdessus (World Water Council, 3rd World Water Forum and Global Water Partnership, March 2003), http://www.worldwatercouncil.org/fileadmin/world_water_council/documents_old/Library/Publications_and_reports/CamdessusSummary.pdf.

representatives from some of the largest private international water businesses, e.g., Veolia, Suez, Ondeo and Thames Water,[14] together with the ex-vice-president of the World Bank, Ismael Serageldin. Other similar commissions and forums have underlined the economic value of water as being complementary (or conflicting) to its social and environmental nature. The debate on the multiple nature of water at a transboundary level also has been registered among water sector trade unions, for example, the October 2002 protest in Uruguay by the *Federación de Funcionarios de las Obras Sanitarias de l'Estado*.[15]

Salman stresses the importance of cross-sectorial and multi-level cooperation citing three treaties, namely, the Amazon Cooperation Treaty, the Treaty for Amazonian Cooperation, the United Nations Economic Commission for Europe (UN/ ECE) Helsinky Convention on the Protection and Use of Transboundary Watercourses and International Lakes, and the Revised Protocol on Shared Watercourses in the Southern African Development Community (SADC).[16] These treaties represent different needs and concerns of the South American and African state parties. Howevr, as Salman underlines, 'despite the differences in the regions, timing and concerns of each of those three legal instruments, a number of common themes still emerge,' namely, 'the participation of and cooperation among the riparians ... as the *sine qua non* for the achievement of the purposes of each of the three instruments.'[17] These reflections show the key role of cooperation beyond boundaries for achieving proper governance of water issues.

These examples show that water issues must not only to be faced through a perspective that goes beyond national frontiers, but also that this perspective

---

14 Veolia Environnement S.A. (the former, until 1998, Compagnie Générale des Eaux and, between 2000 and 2003, Vivendi Environnement) is a French private enterprise providing services like water supply and management. Suez S.A. is a French multinational corporation active in several services, including water supply and management. It was derived from a merger between the Compagnie de Suez and Lyonnaise des Eaux in 1997. Specifically, in order to deal with water supply and waste services, a separate publicly traded company, Suez Environnement, was created. Ondeo Industrial Solutions is a Suez branch created by this latter firm in 2001 to meet a full range of industrial water needs. Thames Water Utilities Ltd. is the largest private utility company managing the public water supply and waste water treatment in the United Kingdom.

15 Sjölander Holland, supra note 6, at 143–144.

16 S. M. A. Salman, 'The Future of International Water Law: Regional Approaches to Shared Watercourses?', *in* M. S. Arsanjani et al. (eds), *Looking to the Future:Essays on International Law in Honor of W. Michael Reisman* (The Hague: Martinus Nijhoff Publishers, 2010), pp. 907–928 at 926.

17 Ibid.

is 'inverted'. This means that water issues must be considered using a 'vertical approach': the attention should be focused not only on water flowing through the rivers, but also on aquifers and vaporized water. This entails focussing attention on the infrastructure surrounding a river, the rock formations unique to a particular aquifer and the materials they are composed of, on air pollution affecting water, and considering the water cycle as a determinant to understanding and rationally handling water issues. Such an evaluation is part of the 'integrated approach' to water management and will be further developed throughout this monograph. A transboundary and integrated approach will be presented as a winning approach on the basis of lessons learnt from Latin America.

A The Right to Water in Latin America: Recognition, Limits, and Criticisms

In this section the development of the right to water in Latin America will be discussed. The process of its insertion in constitutional texts will be illustrated, through legal instruments and other alternative tools, i.e. the jurisprudence of National Courts. A reflection on the opportunity of the choice will follow. Subsequently, the question about the eventual contrast between the concept of the right to water as a human right and water as a privatized good will be analyzed. Finally, the obligations imposed on the state by the particular nature of the right will be underlined.

I *Recognition of the Right to Water and Its Limits*

a A New Right: Presence or Absence in Latin American Constitutions

The RtW is emphatically enunciated in international statements[18] although its very roots are found in national legal experiences. Ensuring a water supply through a public managed service has been justified worldwide with the aim of granting certainty, continuity, uniformity, generality, a certain quality, and a fair price for access to drinkable water. This was just the first step, however, as some states have followed this by formally recognizing the RtW in their constitution. The following overview examines how this process of recognition has occurred, beginning with the acknowledgement that the RtW should be inserted among the 'new rights' or 'fourth generation rights'.

18 For a comprehensive discussion of the development of the right to water see Salman &. McInerney-Lankford, supra note 1.

In order to understand the concept of new rights, it seems useful to review what Bobbio wrote in 1997.[19] He called 'new rights' emerging claims such as the right to live in a non-polluted environment and the right to preserve one's genetic makeup. Bobbio discussed the hypothesis that such rights would be a part of the category of 'fourth generation rights'. These rights would be new social expectations arising from new needs or from the awareness of already existing needs. In addition, new threats to already existing needs may give rise to fourth generation rights.

Among the new rights, distinctions can be drawn in order to categorize them: those that have been endorsed in constitutional statements and are being effectively implemented, and accepted by all the stakeholders as long as they do not impinge on the interests of economic and political powers; those that, in spite of having received formal recognition in national or international texts, are weak and ineffectively implemented; and finally, those emerging new rights, the formal recognition of which has been opposed by certain economic and political stakeholders, because these stakeholders fear the legal and factual consequences that such recognition implies.[20]

The RtW falls into this third category. Only ten constitutions worldwide recognize a direct human RtW.[21] However, several states have indirectly included it in more general environmental human rights. The claims on water resources often began as an answer to attempts to privatize the water supply service and then turned into a claim about the universality, inalienability, and inviolability of the RtW.[22] However, the fact that not all legislators have felt the necessity to formally recognize the RtW in their constitution could represent the first evidence that an explicit statement in a legal text is not necessary if the system already works fairly and efficiently. Indeed, any legal changes should be based on a solid analysis of what good governance means in real experience. This is not to say that the legal recognition is useless; on the contrary, it is of central importance. Legal recognition allows people to claim from the state the protection of the RtW, politically, administratively, and judicially. Therefore, it

---

19 N. Bobbio, *L'età dei diritti* (Torino: Einaudi, 1997).

20 D. Zolo, 'Nuovi diritti e globalizzazione', *Treccani.it L'Enciclopedia Italiana* (2009), http://www.treccani.it/enciclopedia/nuovi-diritti-e-globalizzazione_%28XXI-Secolo%29/.

21 Ecuador (2008), art. 67, ss. 2, 2.15; Ethiopia (1998), art. 90; Gambia (1997), Social Objectives 216, s. 4; Kenya (2010), art. 43; Maldives (2008), s. 23a; Panama (1994), c. 7, art. 118; South Africa (1996), art. 14; Uganda (1995), art. 27b; Uruguay (1967), art. 47; Zambia (1998), art. 112. Source: C. Jeffords, *Constitutional Environmental Human Rights: A Descriptive Analysis of 142 National Constitutions* (Storrs, CT: University of Connecticut, Department of Agricultural and Resource Economics 2013) at 20–21.

22 Zolo, supra note 20.

is indispensable as long as it provides an additional component, i.e. the legal entitlement to claim a right that complements a successful water system.

The wave of recognizing the RtW in constitutions began in the twenty-first century, mainly in developing countries. These fundamental texts are, in general, more recent, more inclined to be replacements, and more susceptible to being influenced by the social and political context.[23] The first element, their recentness, has made them more 'vulnerable' to the international law 'pressure', i.e., to the statements on water protection and water access made at the international level. Indeed, the starting point of the debate on the RtW at the international law level was in the 1970s, corresponding with the 1972 Stockholm United Nations Conference on the Human Environment.[24] The second and third factors, the low durability and the high dependency on the context, have also facilitated the reception of this new right compared to old and consolidated constitutional texts.

With regard to the international influence, there is a mutual contribution between this level and the national level. The domestic framework has been the source of inspiration for international regulation, but often only atter codified by international statements has the RtW been formally inserted in national constitutions.[25] One of the consequences of this reciprocal process is that the principles affirmed at one level are likely to be found at the other level. In this process of constitutionalization of the RtW, civil society often has played an important role, as happened in Porto Alegre, Brazil (see discussion below).

b Longevity of the Constitution and the RtW

The constitutions of Latin America have a very different lifespan compared to those of Western European countries.[26] A study by Ginsburg found that the

---

23 For an overall perspective on Latin American constitutions see G. Negretto, 'The Durability of Constitutions in Changing Environments: A Study on Constitutional Stability in Latin America', paper presented at the American Political Science Association Meeting, Philadelphia, USA, 31 August 2006; G. Negretto, 'Replacing and Amending Constitutions: The Logic of Constitutional Change in Latin America', paper prepared for delivery at the American Political Science Association Meeting, Washington, D.C., USA, 1–4 September 2011.

24 S. M. A. Salman, 'The Human Right to Water and Sanitation: Is the Obligation Deliverable?', *Water International*, Vol. 39(7) (2014), p.2. doi: 10.1080/02508060.2015.986616.

25 M. Rulli & J. B. Justo, *Guía de derechos humanos para empresas: proteger, respetar y remediar: todos ganamos*, (Buenos Aires: Programa de las Naciones Unidas para el Desarrollo, Red Argentina Pacto Global, 2012), at 33.

26 For further details see T. Ginsburg, *The Lifespan of Written Constitutions* (Chicago: University of Illinois, College of Law, 26 December 2007), Table 1 at 30 (constitutional

average lifespan for the Western European fundamental texts was 32 years while the Latin American endured on average 12.4 years, with 15% of them perishing in their first year of existence.[27] The four countries in the world that have the highest number of constitution replacements are all situated in Latin America and the Caribbean. The Dominican Republic is at the top of the list with 32 constitutional texts, followed by Venezuela with 26, Haiti with 24, and Ecuador with 20.[28]

A comprehensive constitutional review, or even a replacement, could be advisable in consideration of an important context variation. Conversely, an enduring constitution proves to better guarantee effective, equitable, and stable democracy.[29] The promulgation of a new constitution marks the beginning of a new constitutional system. Ginsburg's analysis of this phenomenon in Latin America shows that often this change coincides with a transition in the regime of the state.[30] She cites the case of the Chilean Constitution of 1980 as an example.[31]

The Chilean Constitution of 1980 was enacted under the dictatorship of Pinochet, after having received a contested 67% majority of the votes.[32] The text formalized the military dictatorship in the country and granted to General Pinochet a further eight years of absolute power, to be added to the seven years already experienced by the Chilean people. The criticisms on this poll's legitimacy are several, as reported by the Americas Watch Committee[33] and by Alexander.[34] As the latter author stressed, 'the moment that people [could] see [Pinochet's] end and begin to conceive a world without him, his power begins to crumble'.[35]

---

change in Latin America) and Table 2 at 31 (constitutional amendments in Western Europe and Latin America).

27 Ibid., at 48.

28 R. Eustace, 'Fluid Constitutions: A Latin American Phenomenon Council on Hemispheric Affairs', Council on Hemispheric Affairs (3 July 2014), http://www.coha.org/fluid-constitutions-a-latin-american-phenomenon/comment-page-1/.

29 Ginsburg, supra note 26, at 1.

30 Ibid., at 7.

31 Ibid., at 54, fig. 2.

32 W. L. Alexander, 'Enduring Contradictions of the Neoliberal State in Chile,' *in* W. L. Alexander (ed.), *Lost in the Long Transition: Struggles for Social Justice in Neoliberal Chile*, pp. 1–33 (Lanham, MD: Lexington Books, 2009) at 5.

33 Americas Watch Committee, *Chile: Human Rights and the Plebiscite* (New York: Americas Watch Committee, 1988) at 1–33, available at: http://www.corteidh.or.cr/tablas/4478.pdf.

34 Alexander, supra note 32, at 1. For an historical perspective see R. Barros, *Constitutionalism and Dictatorship: Pinochet, the Junta, and the 1980 Constitution* (Cambridge: Cambridge University Press, 2002) at 305–311.

35 Ibid., at 1.

Thus began the so-called "long transition to democracy" in Chile. However, despite this process of re-democratization, the neoliberal economic model developed under the dictatorship endures in Chilean society and is still reflected in its Constitution.

Constitutional texts that are the outcome of such a drastic institutional shift often lack the consensus (an element which implies a certain stability of the constitution over time) of those texts that arise from a democratic process and are more likely to be influenced by the contingencies of the moment. Ginsburg found that constitutions written under democratic regimes last, on average, 17 years longer than those written under authoritarian regimes.[36]

For a constitution to endure, it must be adaptability, i.e., a constitutional system must be able to be modified in response to changes in its context. These changes can be mainly implemented in two ways: formal and informal amendments, the latter deriving from the interpretative power granted through jurisprudence. It appears that there is an inverse relation between formal amendments and constitutional adaptation by judicial interpretation.[37] Moreover, there is a tendency registered in Latin America to what could be called '*de facto* flexibility' through reduced government enforcement of constitutional provisions. The executive, using its discretion over enforcement, can achieve flexibility even when the constitution does not provide for easy ways to be amended.[38]

Another factor allowing longevity is the inclusiveness of a constitution's origins, an element that is more likely to be found in Western European countries' constitutions than in Latin American ones. Indeed, the durability of a constitution depends on the extent to which people 'believe' in it. For the majority of European states, the constitutional text is perceived as a symbol of sovereignty and statehood, while the majority of the Latin American constitutions, mainly those promulgated in the 1800s, are unlikely to find the same level of social recognition.[39] An exception is the Brazilian Constitution of 1988, the drafting

36 Ginsburg, supra note 26, at 18–19.

37 G. Negretto, *The Durability of Constitutions in Changing Environments: Explaining Constitutional Replacement in Latin America*, Working Paper No. 350 (South Bend, IN: University of Notre Dame, Helen Kellogg Institute for International Studies, 2008), http://kellogg.nd.edu/publications/workingpapers/WPS/350.pdf.

38 S. Levitsky & M. V. Murillo, *Building Institutions on Weak Foundations: Lessons from Latin America* (Harvard University and Columbia University, 2012) at 28–29.

For further information, in particular as regards de facto flexibility in labor law, see M. L. Cook, *The Politics of Labor Reform in Latin America: Between Flexibility and Rights* (University Park, PA: Pennsylvania State University Press, 2007).

39 Ginsburg, supra note 26, at 36–37.

of which was characterized by a very intense public involvement and actualized, for example, through the submission of citizen proposals. This highly legitimated text has endured substantially longer than the average of Latin American constitutions.[40]

Ginsburg points to the specificity of the constitutional text as a factor supporting constitutional lifespan, because in a more detailed document the legislator can anticipate future needs that may generate pressure for change.[41] This specificity is often more frequent in Latin American constitutions than in European ones, which are generally characterized by a more concise approach. Many other rights and interests, which European constitutions lack, are instead minutely handled in Latin American texts. For example, the Brazilian Constitution, with 41,404 words at its birth in 1988, is characterized by the constitutionalization of nearly every aspect of public life.

The specificity and excessive length of a constitution threatens its stability over time, as it requires frequent amendments due to the mutable nature of its specific elements. A fitting word which has been used to describe this characteristic of Latin American constitutions is 'fluidity'.[42] The amendment process for fluid constitutions is often difficult due to political divisions within the institutional bodies, and this can lead to the drastic choice of replacement instead of modification.

Another important factor in the longevity of a constitutional text is the strength and effectiveness of the institutions it sets out. Notably, the existence of an entity responsible for constitutional adjudication has central relevance. Also, that entity's effective capability to deliver decisions with *erga omnes* effects is important.[43] In a country provided with such a body, the constitution will be reasonably amendable. On the contrary, where its decisions just have *inter partes* effects, the constitution will be harder to amend, hence it will be more rigid and more likely to need replacement. Among the Latin American countries, only Bolivia and Chile have constitutional adjudication bodies granted with *erga omnes* decisional power. In contrast, in the majority of Western judicial systems have constitutional courts entitled to rule with *erga omnes* effects.

Arguably, the length of a constitutional text is directly proportional with unlawful practices and inversely with the gross domestic product (GDP).

40 Ibid., at 37.

41 Ibid., at 36, 44.

42 Eustace, supra note 28.

43 P. Navia & J. Rios-Figueroa, 'The Constitutional Adjudication Mosaic of Latin America,' *Comparative Political Studies*, Vol. 38(2), (2005), pp. 189–217.

The number of rules, level of bureaucracy, and restrictions required for the enforcement of constitutional rights may incentivize a tendency to elude those prescriptions, even through corrupt means. Evidence of these proportional links is seen in a comparative analysis of the constitutions of Chile and the Dominican Republic. Chile, despite its frequent renewal of its constitution since its founding in 1810 (most of them occurred in the turbulent years after its founding), has had only three constitutional texts since 1833. At the same time, Chile, the Latin American state with the lowest level of corruption, is one of the richest countries in Latin America if we consider the average GDP per capita (as affirmed above, low constitutional replacement is linked with lower corruption and higher GDP). In contrast, the Dominican Republic, founded in 1844, has the highest number of fundamental text's replacements in the world, i.e., 32 in total, and can be considered one of the poorest and most corrupt countries in Latin America.[44]

c Specific Insight into the Latin American Scenario

In 2007, the Office of the High Commissioner for Human Rights (OHCHR) led an in-depth research study on states' positions towards the RtW. In a questionnaire, local governments, intergovernmental organizations, national human rights institutions, non-governmental organizations, the business sector, universities, and individuals were asked to describe the water framework of their context of reference and the policies put in place to grant the RtW.[45] The reports from Latin America showed that the majority of the countries proved to be willing (on paper) to grant the RtW compared to European countries. Does this mean that the RtW is better ensured in Latin America? The following review of the legal framework in LA states suggests that this is not true. Due to its special characteristics, the Chilean framework is discussed in Part C below.

The Constitution of the Republic of Nicaragua, adopted in 1987 and last amended in 2005, contains, in Article 105, the obligation of the state to promote, facilitate, and regulate the provision of basic public services, including water, which is followed by the recognition that the population has an inalienable right to have access to water. This text was the first to recognize access to water as an inalienable right. Among the other constitutions which include such a recognition, are the National Constitution of Panama of 1972 (a case of direct

44 J. L. Cordiero, *Constitutions Around the World: The View from Latin America*, IDE Discussion Paper No. 164 (Chiba, Japan: Institute of Developing Economies, 2008).

45 The response of states' to the OHCHR questionnaire are available at http://www2.ohchr.org/english/issues/water/contributions.htm.

constitutional recognition of the human RtW), last amended in 2004, which affirms in Article 118 the fundamental duty of the state to ensure that people live in a healthy environment free of pollution, where air, water, and food support the proper development of human life.

The Constitution of the Republic of Ecuador of 1998, last amended in 2008, also includes direct constitutional recognition of the RtW. Article 23(20), Chapter 2, grants the right to certain standard of life, to health, food and nutrition, drinking water, among others. The state's committment to the water service is affirmed at Articles 42 and 249, which stress respect of the principles of equity, universality, solidarity, quality, and efficiency in relation to the provision of water. Further on, Section 2, Chapter 5, states that energy sovereignty will neither be achieved at the expense of food sovereignty, nor affect the RtW.

The RtW as a fundamental human right was inserted at Article 47 in the Constitution of the Republic of Uruguay of 1967, last amended in 2004, through a public referendum (the third case of direct constitutional recognition of this human right). Water is defined as a natural resource essential to life, and access to safe water and sanitation is recognized as a basic human right. In addition, the Article affirms that national water and sanitation policies will give priority to the provision of drinking water for the population and that social grounds must prevail over economic grounds. Finally, it states that water integrated in the hydrologic cycle is part of the state's public domain, and that water and sewerage must be provided exclusively and directly by the state.

Another state that has included provisions for granting public control over water in its constitution, this time after civic demonstrations, is Bolivia. Article 107 of its Constitution of 1967, last amended in 2005, confirms that the state controls, regulates, and supervises the exploitation of national goods and the provision of public services. Articles 373–377 of the New Constitution of 2009 recognize water as a fundamental right for life, thus providing an example of the insertion of international water principles into a national text. In Mexico, only as part of 2012 constitutional reforms,[46] was the RtW recognized, together with provisions for a form of civic engagement.

Other Latin American states have recognized the RtW without inserting it into their constitution. Paraguay issued a new National Water Law in 2007[47] that declares all water in the territory of the state as publicly owned and access to water as a fundamental human right. Similarly, the National Constitution of

---

46 Mexico, Decreto por el que se Declara reformado el párrafo quinto y se adiciona un párrafo sexto recorriéndose en su orden los subsecuentes, al artículo 4o. de la Constitución Política de los Estados Unidos Mexicanos, 8 February 2012.

47 Paraguay, Ley de los Recursos Hidricos Del Paraguay n. 3239, 10 July 2007.

Venezuela of 1999, last amended in 2005, in Article 127, charges the state with specific environmental duties, among which water quality is a priority, while the recognition of the RtW is only made at the legislative level. Honduras, in the *Ley Marco del Sector Agua Potable y Saneamiento* of 2003,[48] focuses on the guarantee of the provision of water and ensuring its quality and sustainability.

In Peru, the protection of water is granted under the combined disposition of two laws, the *Ley General de Servicios de Saneamiento* of 1994[49] and the *Ley de Recursos Hídricos*, which also calls for effective civic participation in the water decision-making process. The last water law, as updated in 2009, prohibits water privatization and recognizes water as a human right.[50] Even in Brazil, despite the lack of constitutional recognition, has adopted the *Ley de Saneamento Basico* of 2007,[51] in particular Article 47, which establishes principles and standards for water provision. In Costa Rica, the RtW is granted by the *Principios de la Política Hídrica Nacional* of 2009.[52]

A country that has recognized, but just indirectly, the RtW in its constitution is Colombia. Its fundamental text of 1991, last amended in 2005, does not explicitly confirm the individual right to water and sanitation, but at Article 49 affirms the state's responsibility for public health and the environment and grants public access to services involving public health. The right of access is strengthened by Article 334, which provides for people, particularly those with a low income, effective access to basic services. This right is then confirmed by Article 366, which deals with the fundamental social purposes of the state in managing these services, and by Article 368, which deals with subsidies. A civic campaign to insert the RtW in the constitution and to ensure a vital minimum amount of free water per person failed in 2008. Notwithstanding, a solid jurisprudence of the Constitutional Court affirms the existence of this right (see the discussion below).

Similarly, the 2010 Constitution of the Dominican Republic deals with the obligation of the state to improve alimentation, sanitation services, and hygienic conditions at Article 8. The Guatemalan Constitution of 1985, as amended in 1993, does not explicitly recognize the RtW, but even here there is an indirect commitment of the state to this right under Article 96 where it is affirmed that the state shall improve, among other concerns, the conditions

48 Honduras, Ley Marco del Sector Agua Potable y Saneamiento n.118, 8 October 2003.

49 Peru, Ley General de Servicios de Saneamiento n. 26338, 24 July 1994.

50 Peru, Ley de Recursos Hídricos n. 29338, 31 March 2009.

51 Brazil, Ley de Saneamento Básico n. 11445, 5 January 2007.

52 Costa Rica, text available at http://www.bdlaw.com/assets/htmldocuments/Costa%20Rica%20National%20Water%20Policy.pdf.

of basic environmental sanitation. In Argentina, the Constitution of 1853, last amended in 1994, indirectly recognizes the RtW by providing that efficiency and good quality of public services are fundamental rights. At the constitutional level, an implicit recognition of the RtW has been made through the acknowledgement of the right to a healthy environment. In addition, the efficiency of national remedies has been remarkable as can be observed in the case study of the Matanza-Riachuelo River basin (see Section VI(b)(ii) below).

d Comparing the Latin American Trend with the European RtW Scenario

The Latin American trend is in contrast to Europe where an *explicit* recognition of the RtW in constitution cannot be identified. However, in most European constitutions, the RtW can still be deduced *implicitly* from the right to life, to health and to live in a healthy environment. For example, in the Italian Constitution the RtW could be derived from the right to life, which in turn was deduced by the judges of the Constitutional Court who recognized Article 2 of the Constitution as a 'open article' (*articolo a fattispecie aperta*).[53] This means that this article, due to its broad and elastic formulation, encompasses any further development of the 'material' constitution that leads to a new right, provided that it is linked to existing rights expressly recognized in the 'formal' Constitution. The outcome of this interpretation is the recognition of implicit rights that are indirectly recognized and guaranteed by the existing provisions of the Constitution. Moreover, the RtW could be derived by interpretation from Article 32 of the Italian Constitution, the right to health. It has even been proposed that the RtW derives from Article 27, paragraph 4 of the Italian Constitution,[54] as a result of the Constitutional Reform no. 2/2007,[55] i.e., the abolition of the death penalty. This hypothesis is too extreme to be herein endorsed.

Other states, like the United Kingdom, have officially recognized[56] the RtW although they have not enshrined it in a fundamental text. The United Kingdom has acknowledged the right in response to the launch of the 2006 UN Human Development Report, 'Beyond Scarcity: Power, Poverty and the Global

53 A. Barbera, 'Commento all'art. 2 della Costituzione', *in* G. Branca (ed.), *Commentario della Costituzione italiana* (Bologna: Zanichelli, 1975).

54 S. Staiano, 'Note sul diritto fondamentale all'acqua. Proprietà del bene, gestione del servizio, ideologie della privatizzaizone', *Federalismi.it*, Vol. 5 (2011) at 2.

55 Italy, Riforma Costituzionale, 2 October 2007, n. 2.

56 See 'United Kingdom', The Rights to Water and Sanitation, http://www.righttowater.info/progress-so-far/national-legislation-on-the-right-to-water/#UK.

Water Crises'.[57] The note verbale 313,[58] dated 4 July 2007, by the Permanent Mission of Great Britain and Northern Ireland to the United Nations and Other International Organizations in Geneva endorsed the human right to water as deriving from the interpretation of Article 11 of the International Covenant on Economic, Social and Cultural Rights (ICESCR).[59] Moreover, it affirmed the following principles: namely, that the priority for human use shall always be granted in the water decision-making process and that the RtW must be ensured for each individual without discrimination. In addition, the Note describes the state's engagement in helping to achieve the RtW in developing countries through the actions of the Department for International Development (DFID). In particular, the 2006 White Paper of DFID, 'Eliminating World Poverty: Making Governance Work for the Poor', set out guidelines for actions in this regard.[60]

With regard to the broader European framework, the European Union (EU) has been a determining element in the formulation of water legislation through fundamental Charter statements (which indirectly recognize the RtW),[61] adoption of regulations and national implementation of directives (this topic is discussed further in Part B below).[62] However, there is no formal recognition of the RtW in any fundamental text of the EU. Nonetheless, the EU citizens have

57 See United Nations Development Programme, *Human Development Report 2006: Beyond Scarcity: Power, Poverty and the Global Water Crisis* (New York: UNDP, 2006).

58 Text of the note verbale 313 is available at: http://www2.ohchr.org/english/issues/water/contributions/United%20Kingdom.pdf.

59 The International Covenant on Economic, Social and Cultural Rights (ICESCR), was adopted and opened for signature, ratification and accession by General Assembly resolution 2200A (XXI) of 16 December 1966, entry into force 3 January 1976. For more information on the interpretation of Article 11 ICESCR see S. M. A. Salman, *The Human Right to Water—Challenges of Implementation*, in *Proceedings of the Annual Meeting of the American Society of International Law, Confronting Complexity*, Vol. 106 (Cambridge: Cambridge University Press, 2012) at 44–46.

60 Secretary of State for International Development (United Kingdom), *Eliminating World Poverty: Making Governance Work for the Poor, A White Paper on International Development* (July 2006), https://www.gov.uk/government/uploads/system/uploads/attachment_data/file/272330/6876.pdf.

61 Charter of Fundamental Rights of the European Union, 2012/C 326/02 (26 October 2012). In particular, Article 2 (the right to life), Article 35 (protection of human health), Article 36 (access to services of general economic interest), Article 37 (environmental protection and sustainable development), and Article 38 (consumer protection) of the.

62 The general framework for water regulation has been provided by Council Directive 1998/83/EC of 3 November 1998 on the quality of water intended for human consumption, OJ L 330, 5 December 1998 and Directive 2000/60/EC of the European Parliament and of the Council of 23 October 2000 establishing a framework for Community action in

been proactive in water matters. In April 2012, a European Citizens' Initiative,[63] a tool introduced under the Lisbon Treaty to encourage greater democratic involvement of citizens in European affairs, was launched with the aim of calling attention to the RtW.

Conclusively, it is opportune to reflect on the reason why Latin America has been so active in the constitutionalization of the RtW compared to Europe. First, as said above, the more recent nature of developing countries' constitutions, as well as their higher susceptibility to being revised or replaced, has played a central role. The new right has been more easily inserted in these fundamental texts due to these features. In addition, it may be assumed that the presence of drought, which is more pressing in Latin America, has influenced this 'race' to recognize the RtW. However, it can be argued that some European areas face water scarcity,[64] such as the southern part of Italy, but the circumstance in the European states has not led to such constitutional recognition.

While water shortages are more common nowadays, they are not 'new' to the extent that it has been a plague on humanity since its origin. Therefore, the very basic question is why an ancient concern, that is, water scarcity and security of access to water, only recently has led legislators to take into account its guarantee through legal instruments. Arguably, although this juridical position (the RtW granted on a daily base and according to a certain quality and price standard) has always existed, what has radically changed is the context: the new menaces to the RtW, namely, the unequal 'sale' of water to private enterprises, the excessive exploitation of the resource, and new chemical products leading to additional and unpredictable forms of pollution, are a warning to national legislators that a stronger protection, maybe constitutional, is opportune.[65]

There are two fundamental ways meet these new demands: constitutional reform and extension of existing provisions, depending on the elasticity of those dispositions and, importantly, through judicial interpretation. Obviously,

---

the field of water policy, OJ L 327, 22 December 2000, as amended by Decision 2455/2001/EC, Directive 2008/32/EC and Directive 2009/31/EC.

63 See Communication from the Commission on the European Citizens' Initiative 'Water and sanitation are a human right! Water is a public good, not a commodity!', COM(2014) 177 final, 19 March 2014. The European Citizens' Initiative allows at least one million citizens of the EU, coming from at least seven member states, to call on the European Commission to propose legislation on matters of EU competence. It is the first ever participatory democracy instrument at the EU level. Since its launch in April 2012, more than five million citizens have signed up to over 20 different initiatives.

64 It is opportune to bear in mind that the European states are in general considered areas with a high level of water availability and water consumption.

65 Staiano, supra note 54, at 4.

including a constitutional provision as enforceable law produces a stronger responsibility for policy-makers to subsequently implement the right and allocate resources for that purpose. The same obligation does not have the same legal force if it derives from judicial interpretation. The question raised by this 'alternative' approach to the explicit recognition is whether such a statement is suitable and desirable or, on the contrary, the 'crystallization' of this right in a legal text could—in some instances—limit its potential to be more flexibly regulated by the legislator.

Moreover, a constitutional statement may threaten other constitutional rights, which will have to be balanced with this new right.[66] Tega identified this new right as one of the main causes of the actual crisis that affects the 'traditional' nationwide protected rights. These latter rights, indeed, are challenged by the universalism of 'cooperative constitutionalism', which goes beyond national borders and is witnessed by the growing role of international courts.[67] The multi-level protection benefits the individual providing him/her with several venues to plead for his/her rights but, at the same time, the legitimacy and accountability of national courts risk to be weakened. However, at the same time, the constitutional recognition of the RtW could be a useful tool precisely to allow this balance among constitutionally recognized values and the RtW, and to prevent the abusive claim of this right.

The constitutional recognition of the right could lead to its exploitation or over-use if the intrinsic limit of the RtW is not considered: water is a limited resource. For this reason, people cannot claim their RtW if that implies that they will use more water than needed, preventing their neighbors or future generations from getting access to water. In this case, people have the duty to balance their right with neighbors' and future generations' right to life and with environmental concerns in order to exercise the RtW in a wise and sustainable way. Therefore, a central concern is represented by the debate on the position this right shall occupy, either explicitly or implicitly recognized.

All in all, the RtW should be considered as a 'collective but at the same time individual fundamental right'[68] placed among the social rights of a model constitution. Furthermore, it could be considered even a 'functional right'[69] as long as it is indispensable for the development of other rights, like the right to

---

66 Ibid., at 2.

67 D. Tega, *I diritti in crisi. Tra Corti nazionali e Corte europea di Strasburgo* (Milan: Università degli Studi di Milano Bicocca, 2012).

68 Rulli & Justo, supra note 25, at 22.

69 Statement of Felipe Tapia Valencia, VII Jornadas de Derecho ambiental, 15 October 2014, Santiago de Chile.

life, to health, for economic development, and even for education. Indeed, in countries facing water scarcity, a considerable part of the population, mainly the most vulnerable ones, i.e. women and children, spend their time collecting water, often walking for hours, time that could be better spent without this daily obligation.

e The Right to Water in the Jurisprudence of Latin American Courts

In those countries that lack an explicit recognition of the RtW, the alternative outcome has been a flourishing of constitutional jurisprudence in defense of the right. On one side, Latin American courts have proven to be active in the application of the principle of proportionality[70] to decisions related to water. This is done in order to verify the legitimacy of eventual restrictions to the right, the adequacy of tools used, the finality of the act, and the proportion between the objective achieved and the sacrifice caused. 'Not more than the necessary', with constant attention to the balance among different interests, has been the guiding principle.

The Republic of Colombia, even if it has not achieved the constitutional recognition of the RtW, shows jurisprudence that somehow replaces the fundamental text's guarantee.[71] From the constitutional statement on the state commitments towards the public service, i.e., their efficiency, generality and good quality, the legislative and judicial powers are the basis for the establishment of the right. In particular, at the legislative level, *Ley* 142/1994 provides for the continuity and minimum quality of water supply.[72] At the judicial level, the Constitutional Court of Colombia has dealt with the possibility of suspending access to water in response to non-payment by the user through its decisions of 2010 (no. 614 and 717) and of 2011 (no.740).[73]

In these judgements, the Court recognizes the legitimacy of the suspension as an efficient instrument to stimulate users' payment and to develop a '*cultura de pago*', which often is low in LA countries. However, the rights of the water provider must be limited in order to avoid infringements of fundamental values. First, the right to be heard should be granted to the user, in order to justify the reason for his/her non-payment. Secondly, some institutions or

70 Rulli & Justo, supra note 25, at 22.

71 Ibid., at 34; G. McGraw, 'Defining and Defending the Right to Water and its Minimum Core: Legal Construction and the Role of National Jurisprudence', *Loyola University Chicago International Law Review*, Vol. 8(2) (2011) pp. 127–204.

72 Colombia, Régimen de los Servicios Públicos Domiciliarios, Ley n.142, 11 July 1994.

73 Corte Constitucional de Colombia, Sentencias T-614/2010, T-717/2010 and T-740/2011. Text of judgements available at http://www.corteconstitucional.gov.co/relatoria/.

specific places (e.g., schools, prisons, and hospitals), as well as specific categories of constitutionally protected people, are excluded from the provider's right of suspension. In those cases, the interruption of water supply can lead to more severe consequences than those caused by the lack of payment: therefore, the intervention would prove to be disproportionate because it generates sacrifices more important than the related benefits (T-614/2010, T-717/2010 and T-740/2011).

The Court has been 'pragmatic' to issue a solution that balances the two interests, i.e., the grant of a vital minimum and the need to recover the water cost for the supplier. The Court stated that if the non-payment has occurred for two consecutive periods, the provider shall inform the user of his/her obligation and accord a certain time to comply, also allowing the possibility of flexible payments in relation to the user's economic capacity. If, despite these remedies, an accord is not achieved, but the user proves that he/she has an economic situation justifying the non-fulfillment of the obligation, the enterprise will, at its own expense, insert a 'restrictor of water flow' that ensures a minimum of 50 litres of water per person/per day. Alternatively, the enterprise has to verify the presence of a public fountainhead nearby before suspending service. This can be considered one of the best examples of the grant of the vital minimum of water to every individual through a judicial solution (T-614/2010, T-717/2010 and T-740/2011).[74]

The Colombian Constitutional Court has also affirmed that the RtW implies certain obligations for the state. The first is the implemention of an effective public policy on water based on a structured program inspired by the logic of equity and progressiveness. Secondly, the first priority of this public polity should be the achievement of a widespread access to water. Thirdly, the decision-making process involving water governance should allow forms of democratic participation (T-595/2002 and T-418/2010).[75]

In line with this enlightened approach, in more recent years other rulings have stressed concepts like the vital minimum (see further below), the human right nature of the right to water, and the standards of good quality. For example, Sentencia T-641/15 discussed the threshold of prejudice to the RtW justifying the recourse to the judiciary, and linked the RtW to the right to life and to dignity.[76] Moreover, Sentencia T-139/16 recognized the violation of the RtW and forced the *Alcaldía de Bucaramanga* to ensure a vital minimum to

---

74 On this topic see also Corte Constitucional de Colombia, Sentencias T-539/1993, T-1104/2005, T-091/2010, T-381/2009, T-418/2010, and T-143/2010.

75 Corte Constitucional de Colombia, Sentencias T-595/2002 and T-418/2010.

76 Corte Constitucional de Colombia, Sentencia T-641/15.

the claimants.[77] The objective and subjective nature of the fundamental right to water is stressed in Sentencia T-131/16.[78] Lastly, in Sentencia T-100/17, the Court reflected on the three facets of the RtW: (i) as a vital and valuable resource for the environment, nature and living beings; (ii) as an essential resource for the subsistence of humanity that is materialized in a collective right and is provided through public services; and (iii) as a fundamental right enjoying the enforceability of individual rights.[79]

The Supreme Court of Justice of Costa Rica, in its decision no. 9629 of 2002,[80] considers, like the Colombian Constitutional Court, that the suspension of water service is a violation of the RtW. Notwithstanding, it admits the possibility to suspend the provision for non-payment, but only under two conditions: a duty to inform the user about his/her debt to the provider and the fulfillment of the obligation to install a public water fountain close to the defaulting user. What is missing is the requirement of the vital minimum that was affirmed by the Colombian Constitutional Court (T-614/2010, T-717/2010 and T-740/2011).

The concept of the vital minimum, as stated in the decisions of the constitutional courts of Colombia can also be found in the ruling of the Argentinean *Cámara de Apelaciones en lo Contencioso Administrativo y Tributario de la Ciudad de Buenos Aires* (Case "*Asociación Civil por la Igualdad y la Justicia*" of 2007 no. 20898/0).[81] This case affirmed the local (i.e., municipal) government obligation to guarantee through tanker trucks the provision of drinkable water to a marginal area of Buenos Aires in order to achieve continuity and equality in water access. This ruling was considered one of the first steps towards the development of the basic content of the RtW. Another important judgment on the RtW was delivered by the Supreme Court of Buenos Aires, which efficiently settled a water dispute that arose at the local level (see Section VI(b)(ii) below for the case study onthe Matanza-Riachuelo River basin).[82] Similarly, the Constitutional Court of Peru, lacking constitutional recognition of the RtW, has drawn, in its decision no. 6546/2006,[83] from

77 Corte Constitucional de Colombia, Sentencia T-139/16.

78 Corte Constitucional de Colombia, Sentencia T-131/16.

79 Corte Constitucional de Colombia, Sentencia T-100/17.

80 Corte Suprema de Justicia de Costa Rica, Sentencia 9629/2002.

81 Argentina, Cámara de Apelaciones en lo Contencioso Administrativo y Tributario de la Ciudad de Buenos Aires, Causa Nº 20898/0, Asociación Civil por la Igualdad y la Justicia c/ GCBA s/ amparo, 18 July 2007.

82 Argentina, Sentencia M. 1569. XL/2006, *MENDOZA Beatriz Silvia y Otros C/ ESTADO NACIONAL y Otros S/ Daños y Perjuicios* (daños derivados de la contaminación ambiental del Río Matanza-Riachuelo).

83 Corte Constitucional de Perù, Sentencia no. 6546/2006.

the tenets of human dignity and defined it as an implicit fundamental right, forming the basis of a democratic state oriented to the welfare of its inhabitants. Subsequently, the right has been legally recognized in the New Water Law of 2009,[84] following the spirit of this judicial decision.

A particular sensibility was shown by the Constitutional Court of Bolivia in its ruling no. 684 of 2010, which analyzes the rise of the RtW debate as a reaction to a market-oriented tendency in water management.[85] The Court affirmed that the historic origin of the RtW had its roots in the ongoing 'War for Water'. It makes an implicit reference to the facts that surround the conflict on water in the Bolivian city of Cochabamba (see below). Furthermore, in its decision no. 1106/2010-R, the Court declared that the RtW belongs to every individual if only for the fact to stay alive.[86] For this reason, it cannot be privatized or subjected to the logic of the market, otherwise the water itself will be merchandised.

More recently, the Bolivian Constitutional Court (Sentencia 1230/2016-S3) reasserted the nature of the RtW as a fundamental right and its double nature that—according to the Court—would entail two constitutional dimensions.[87] The first would be the nature of a fundamental individual right. The second regards a collective right, as recognized both in constitutional and in international instruments, whose protection must not respond to an anthropocentric and exclusive vision. In this sense, the individual right to water and the exercise of this right cannot be arbitrary, but should be balanced in consideration of the interests of the community at large and of the scarcity of the resource.

In recent years, the Latin American courts remain active in discussing the human right to water. An example is the crucial pronunciation issued on 26 November 2014, by the Supreme Court of Justice of Mexico (ruling no. 49/2014).[88] In its decision, the Court revoked a previous judgment of the Collegiate Court of the 18th District of Morelos. The latter court determined that the Municipality of Xochitepec had fulfilled its obligations on the human right to water and sanitation by placing a hose with an irregular and scarce flow of water at the claimant's home.[89]

---

84 Peru, Ley de Recursos Hídricos no. 29338, 31 March 2009.

85 Corte Constitucional de Bolivia, Sentencia 684/2010.

86 Corte Constitucional de Bolivia, Sentencia 1106/2010-R.

87 Corte Constitucional de Bolivia, Sentencia 1230/2016-S3.

88 Suprema Corte de Justicia de la Nación, Sentencia 49/2014, 26 November 2014 (México).

89 J. M. Portuguez & V. Dubois Cisneros, *Implementación del derecho humano al agua en América Latina, Proceso Regional de las Américas Sub-región América del Sur, VII Foro Mundial del Agua, Corea* (Caracas: Corporación Andina de Fomento, 2015).

The Supreme Court of Justice stressed that constitutional and international obligations granting the human right to water prescribe that each person should receive between 50 and 100 litres of water per day. According to the Supreme Court, the Collegiate Court failed to contemplate these internationally recognized standards. Moreover, the Supreme Court claimed that the lower court confused the human right to water with the human right to sanitation, which substantially differ in nature and scope. Consequently, the Supreme Court revoked the judgment of the Collegiate Court and forced the Municipality to grant a minimum of 120 litres per day per person. This formula was determined by dividing the total volume of water conceded to the Municipality concession by the number of its inhabitants. Furthermore, the ruling clarified that access to drinking water cannot be confused with the right to sanitation. The two rights have been guaranteed differently, and granting one of them does not ensure compliance with the other. This decision can be considered remarkable because it demonstrates the ongoing process of definition and clarification of the RtW and its recognition in positive law.

II *The Role of Law in Resolving Water Management Issues*

The actual status of the debate on water in Latin America is rather controversial. Therefore, it is complex to outline 'the just role' that the law should play in handling water issues. According to relevant authors active in the water debate,[90] the legal arena is not the right place to deal with water issues. It is asserted that the legislative tools for water regulation are often the outcome of compromise and negotiations among various stakeholders. High costs and a considerable investment of time are required to achieve a compromise within and outside legislative assemblies. Hence, it is claimed that the law often does not reflect the rapid evolution of the problems and conflicts associated with the use of water and with a river basin's management. On the contrary, the development of these issues requires a prompt and easily achievable answer.[91]

The doctrine also points out that the process of amending a law that deals with water issues, all the more so if it is the outcome of shaky political compromises, often results in a complex and long process. Indeed, any variation has to be subjected to a new approval by the various components of the legislative process, causing slowness, transaction costs, and inefficiencies. Instead, in

90 A. Massarutto, *Privati dell'Acqua?* (Bologna: il Mulino 2011); Sjölander Holland, supra note 6, at 26; C. Jampaglia & E. Molinari, *Salvare l'Acqua* (Milan: Feltrinelli Editore, 2010); F. Segerfeldt, *Acqua in vendita?* (2003), (trad.it. Torino: IBL Libri, 2011).

91 A. C. Dourojeanni, *Reformas a las leyes de agua en América Latina* (Santiago de Chile: Fundación Chile, 2014b).

order to properly deal with the mutability of water matters, flexible tools are advisable.

The doctrine's last concern regards the fact that legal provisions are neither always based on a generalized political and economic support, nor always result from a participatory process that engages and represents the preferences of civil society.[92] Evidence of this verification comes from reflections[93] on the attempted reform of the Chilean Water Code discussed in the Chilean Parliament (see Part C). Innovative proposals are often derailed by political propaganda, and this makes it difficult to create real modifications.[94] Instead, water reforms should be rooted in the civil society's will and should represent the outcome of an inclusive decision-making process.

The core of the doctrine is not focused on the law itself but on its contents: norms are central to setting up the water regulatory framework, but they must be targeted towards specific objectives and planning for resource management at the local level.[95] From the analysis of this theory it is evident that it is not always necessary to adopt general and abstract norms for solving water issues. Instead, the water debate could be faced with a more specific approach, namely, the river basin unit approach (as discussed in Part B).

The above illustrated doctrine has the merit of answering the problematic question of why countries, which have adopted similar legal water-related provisions, often face different issues while countries having diverse legislation face similar water problems. Furthermore, the doctrine focuses the attention on the need of a pragmatic approach to set up water regulations.

However, the denial of the role of the law in handling the water issue lacks the necessary balance that is extremely important in defining water policies. The exclusion of legislators from the debate is as detrimental as the exclusion of civil society or the private sector. The legislative branch holds

---

92 A. C. Dourojeanni, *Gestión integrada por Cuencas: una elección politica de gobernanza sobre territories delimitados por razones naturales* (Quito: Fundación Chile, 2010); Organisation for Economic Co-operation and Development (OECD), *Key Messages and Draft Principles on Stakeholder Engagement*, Draft for Working Group Consultation, 18 April 2014, in preparation for the 3rd Meeting of the OECD Water Governance Initiative, 28–29 April 2014, Madrid, Spain.

93 A. C. Dourojeanni & A. Jouravlev, *El Código de Aguas de Chile: entre la ideología y la realidad* (Santiago de Chile: CEPAL, 1999); C. Szigeti Correa, *Reformas Constitucionales en materia de agua y reformas al Código de Aguas*, Comisiones de Trabajo, Proyectos de Ley y Mociones Parlamentarias presentadas a tramitación (Santiago de Chile: Edición Sara Larraín, Programa Chile Sustentable, 2013).

94 Dourojeanni, supra note 91, at 6.

95 Dourojeanni, supra note 91.

a central position because it represents the citizens' will in consideration of the electoral mandate received from the people. This is not to say that that every modification to the actual water framework should derive from the law in order to respect the citizens' mandate. As discussed by Dourojeanni in his study on Latin American water law reforms,[96] a number of authors[97] attributes the failures of the water system to the legal framework regulating such system. Bauer believes that the central point lays in changing the law, even when the change should be made in governance.[98] These latter arguments do not reflect the reality of the mismatch between the legal framework in force and the actual functioning of a water system.

Ultimately, the frequent discrepancy between what is proclaimed by the law—*the law on the books*—and reality—*the law in action*—(see *infra* in this Part and Parts B and C) demonstrates that the decisions of legislative assemblies is not always reflected in the reality. Therefore, legislators should be aware of this phenomenon and try to plan legal strategies that are the closest possible to the factual needs of the society. The balance between the norms proclaimed in theory and the law in execution is exactly the goal to which water policy-makers must aim.

III *The Suitability of the Judicial System to Settle Water Disputes*

It is now important to consider whether the judicial system represents the most suitable place to deal with controversies on water allocation and the environmental consequences of water use. The theory discussed above by Dourojeanni and Jouravlev (which is critical towards the law) firmly challenges

96 A. C. Dourojeanni, 'Reflexiones sobre los cambios en la legislación y organización para la gestión del agua en América Latina', Iagua (29 September 2014), http://www.iagua.es/blogs/axel-dourojeanni/reflexiones-cambios-legislacion-y-organizacion-gestion-agua-america-latina.

97 J. B. Justo, *El derecho humano al agua y al saneamiento frente a los Objetivos de Desarrollo del Milenio* (Santiago de Chile: CEPAL, 2013); Staiano, supra note 54; J-F. Vergès, *Experiencias relevantes de marcos institucionales y contratos en agua potable y alcantarillado* (Santiago de Chile: CEPAL, , 2010); J. Brown, 'How Chile Might Leave the "Chilean Model" Behind: President Bachelet's Proposal to Reform the Country's Famously Laissez-Faire Water Laws', KBH Center for Energy, Law & Business, University of Texas at Austin (3 July 2014), http://kbhenergycenter.utexas.edu/2014/07/03/how-chile-might-leave-the-chilean-model-behind-president-bachelets-proposal-to-reform-the-countrys-famously-laissez-faire-water-laws/.

98 Speech of C. Bauer, VII Jornadas de Derecho ambiental, 15 October 2014, Facultad de Derecho, Universidad de Chile, Santiago de Chile.

this choice as well.[99] The authors' main concerns are, firstly, the high costs that judicial processes generate for both the plaintiff and the defendant. Moreover, they point out that lawsuits often last for long time, making litigants endure in a situation of uncertainty, which prejudices them.

The consideration of these factors often dissuades individuals from claiming their rights before courts. In particular, a subject whose interests have been affected by externalities of little importance usually prefers not to start a lawsuit because he/she is not going to be able to afford the cost of the proceedings. It is important to note that often those who suffer violations of their rights to water and to live in a health environment are the weakest members of the society. For example, farmers, indigenous communities, and water companies' workers are likely to see their claims rejected because the resources are owned by more powerful stakeholders. Indeed, the financial resources availabile to resource owners and their political connections often make them the winning party in court trials.

Lastly, Dourojeanni and Jouravlev underline that courts do not aim to maximize the common gain through the achievement of a compromise between the various interests. On the contrary, judicial resolutions tend to support only one party's claims, the party having the law on its side. This way of operating, they say, hinders the achievement of the highest benefit possible for both the parties, while it maximizes only the profit of the victorious stakeholder.

This theory undoubtedly has elements of truth, the high cost of trials and the prejudices generated by the slowness of justice, are evidence of this reality. However, it is reprehensible to exclude an important component of the state, the judicial branch, from the debate on water. As explained in this chapter, Latin American courts have been extremely prolific in defining guarantees for the individual regarding the right to a safe environment by establishing the right to water. The courts have often provided safeguards for users against a state's negligence and companies' misbehavior.

For these latter considerations, the role of the courts in handling water matters should not be denied. Arguably, it could be useful to search for alternative ways to settle disputes, like arbitration, when it is possible and parties are willing to do so. However, courts should hold a central position in defining the case law for water issues because the judicial body represents an indispensable tool to actualize legislation and adapt it to the needs of the changing reality.

99 Dourojeanni & Jouravlev, supra note 93, at 61.

IV *Is the Concept of the Right to Water as a Human Right in Antithesis with Privatization?*

The multi-level debate on water management often reflects the opportunity to preserve the RtW through a public provision and investigates the possibility to grant this right through private management. Following the orientation of the 1992 Dublin Conference, numerous authors, among which it is worth to quote Salman and McInerney-Lankford[100] and Segerfeldt,[101] advanced the argument that the recognition of water as a human right does not prevent the possibility of privatizing the service.

First, apart from the recognition of the RtW, the afore-mentioned argument is based on democracy: if the decision to privatize has been taken through a democratic process, then privatization cannot be considered undemocratic because people have chosen it. Furthermore, water provided privately can be distributed on an equal basis.

Secondly, it is argued that defining the RtW as a human right does not necessarily imply that its provision shall be run by the state if the private sector can offer a better service, due to its higher technical knowledge, economic resources, and managerial skills. Therefore, it is perfectly reasonable to attribute both a social and an economic value to water: once the social needs have been satisfied, water could be managed as an economic good, as affirmed by Kasrils, former South African Minister of Water Affairs and Forestry.[102] From the recognition of the economic value of water, it can be derived that water shall have a price. However, what is an acceptable cost in consideration of its social nature? The adoption of a dual tariff has been proposed. One tariff would be set for full cost recovery for the majority of the users, while a second tariff would only aim to ensure sustainable cost recovery and would be intended for that part of society which, because of its economic conditions, cannot afford the full price.[103]

Against this opinion stand those who support the provision of water for free, relying on the concept of the vital minimum (50 litres of good quality water per day/per person is recognized as the amount necessary for a decent life) developed by the World Health Organization.[104] This amount, according

100 Salman & McInerney-Lankford, supra note 1.

101 Segerfeldt, supra note 90, at 157–160, 163.

102 Statement of Ronald Kasrils, Forum on Investments in Africa, Johannesburg, South Africa, 7–9 April 2003.

103 R. Petrella, *Un anno di lotte politiche per l'acqua*, in R. Petrella & R. Lembo (eds.), *L'Italia che fa acqua* (Rome: Intra Moenia, 2010), at 152–153.

104 World Health Organization (WHO), *Guidelines for Drinking-water Quality* (Geneva: WHO, 2011).

to relevant authors as Jampaglia and Molinari, should be ensured daily and for free to everyone. They propose eliminating water wastefulness through penalties applied for abusive and excessive water consumption. According to this second approach, water saving and the RtW are two principles that the free market approach cannot guarantee.[105]

In Part B below, the arguments presented here are futher developed by analysing the RtW 'in context', that is, beyond its abstract recognition in a constitution. The discussion focuses on the main LA water management systems in light of the need to apply the RtW to existing water management models. The discussion will show that there are outstanding private models ensuring the RtW, as well as failing public models that harm the RtW. Therefore, the correlation between the public model and guarantees for the respect of the RtW is not straightforward.

V *Obligations of the State towards the Right to Water*

The concepts of water as a human necessity or water as a human right entail a very different pretension that the citizen has towards the state. In the first case, the citizen has a passive role: he/she should receive from the state the necessary tools to access water of sufficient quantity and quality, if unable to do so on his/her own, but cannot claim this pretension in front of any institutional body. On the contrary, in the second case, he/she is entitled to demand that the state comply with the obligation to ensure the RtW before a judicial body, exercising an active role. This is the main reason why often states are unwilling to formally recognize this right. Once the terminology of a 'right' is used, then the question of the basic content of the right rises the central issue.[106]

The basic obligations linked to the RtW have been developed since its implicit recognition as a right in the ICESCR.[107] The turning point occurred in 2002 with the publication of the General Comment no. 15, on the right to water, by the Committee on Economic, Social and Cultural Rights. The Committee through this General Comment provided a guide to the interpretation of the relevant provision contained in the ICESCR.[108]

McGraw underlined the minimum components of the RtW, whose realization is assigned to the responsibility of the state.[109] They can be recapitulated

105 Jampaglia & Molinari, supra note 90, at 144–146.

106 Rulli & Justo, supra note 25, at 26.

107 ICESCR, supra note 59.

108 Salman & McInerney-Lankford, supra note 1, p. 4.

109 G. McGraw, 'Defining and Defending the Right to Water and its Minimum Core: Legal Construction and the Role of National Jurisprudence,' Loyola *University Chicago International Law Review*, Vol. 8(2) (2011), pp. 127–204.

as follows, also in light of the constitutional developments registered in Latin American and presented above:

- Non-discrimination in access to water, i.e., an equal distribution of water, avoiding advantages to the most powerful groups, and providing for instruments to achieve substantial equality in water access.
- The commitment to ensure a vital minimum of water to each individual. It must be noted that a state that is not able to fulfill this obligation will have to demonstrate that it has implemented all the resources available in an attempt to ensure this minimum as a priority. In other words, the state must demonstrate the material impossibility of ensuring the RtW. The jurisprudence of the Colombian Constitutional Court has clearly affirmed this principle.[110] The vital minimum comprises a settled quantity (50 litres per person/per day), a standard quality (technical requirement), and a maximum distance to the water source.
- The state has a duty to implement water governance in a way that facilitates users' participation and transparency in the decision-making process.
- The provision of assistance from richer states to developing states in order to allow every state to comply with these obligations.
- The progressive nature of these obligations means that they must be considered in the framework of a constant process of improving water users' conditions: once the minimum is achieved for everyone, the state must take further measures to widen beyond that minimum.

An example of the drastic consequences that follow from a state's compliance with these principles is illustrated through the case study of Cochabamba, Bolivia (see VI(b)(iii) below) and the review of the Chilean highly privatized water scenario (see Part C). The state's fulfilment of its duties towards its citizens with regards to ensuring the RtW are therefore crucial to ensuring that, regardless of whether there is privatization or public management of the water system, water is provided and managed as a human right.

110 Corte Constitucional de Colombia, Sentencia C-251/1997: '*existe un contenido esencial de los derechos económicos y sociales, el cual se materializa en los derechos mínimos de subsistencia para todos, sea cual fuere el nivel de desarrollo económico. Por ende, se considera que existe una violación a las obligaciones internacionales si los Estados no aseguran ese mínimo vital, salvo que existan poderosas razones que justifiquen la situación*'.

VI *Why is the Water Debate a Core Issue in the Politics of a Country?*

a Water Issues and State Stability

Water concerns are growing in importance on the political agenda of several countries, for example, the highly debated reform of the Chilean Water Code. In the case studies discussed below, the consequences of water conflicts and water insecurity will be presented as detrimental to state stability itself. The reasons for this circumstance are linked to the essentiality of water for the political, social and economic well-being of a country. Indeed, among other roles, water is indispensable to satisfying social needs, guaranteeing biodiversity of the environment, and ensuring economic growth.

Water is a strategic topic for policy-makers; however, in the Latin American context, scarce political attention is reserved for the topic. The demand for more attentive and informed political debate on water policies is becoming more and more urgent in Latin America. Governmental resistance to substantial changes, combined with an insufficient and non-transparent dialogue with civil society, in the long term may affect substantially the prosperity of LA countries and their social and economic growth.[111]

b Case Studies

Three case studies from Latin America offer deeper insight into the topics discussed above.

i *The Right to Water and Civic Participation: The Case of Porto Alegre, Brazil*

The city of Porto Alegre, in Brazil, is an outstanding example in the Brazilian context: it has the lowest child mortality rate in the country and its development is comparable to that of a developed country. In particular, its water system is one of the most efficient in the region, presenting at the same time the lowest tariff for water supply. The management of the water sector is in the hands of the municipality. What are the key factors for this success? First, a crucial element has been the assignment of the water service's management to an independent body that is functionally and financially autonomous. A good balance between the economic sustainability of the system and social equity seems to be another key factor. Around one-quarter of the income is re-invested to improve infrastructure. In addition, tariffs are equalized through tax exemptions.

What seems to be the very special feature of the system is the degree of civic involvement. A panel of technicians and users' representatives supervise the

111 Sáez-Muñoz, supra note 4, at 296.

governance of the water service.[112] This panel has veto power on water decisions affecting the common good. Moreover, the inhabitants of the city are constantly informed about the developments and management of the water system through the release of relevant documents (e.g. plans for future investments). This constant monitoring by the service users is the crucial element that makes the system efficient. It also implies a double commitment: the provider allows the people to control it giving them the information necessary to do so; in turn, the users commit themselves to analyzing the documents in order to exercise their power consciously.

It must be noted that, at the national level, Brazil also engages civil society in water decisions.[113] The importance of direct citizens' participation was translated from the local to the national level through the City Statute.[114] This statute represents an innovative legal framework that brought the local experiences on popular decision-making to the national level.

Subsequently, in 2007, the Law on Sanitation was issued.[115] This law is the result of a compromise among the interests of the various stakeholders who participated in the political discussion preceeding the drafting of every new law and, consequently, reflects the needs of civil society. Its precursor is the 1997 Law on Water Resources.[116] This latter law explicitly recognizes water as a common good and affirms the priority of human consumption in cases of water scarcity. Moreover, it not only stresses the importance of civic participation, but it also pays attention to the interests of future generations through the definition of mechanisms aimed at sustainable water use. On the basis of this law, a participatory consultation process was directed to civil society and the National Water Resources Plan was approved in 2006. Part of the Plan deals with the topic of civic engagement in water governance, specifically the issue of marginalized groups and their access to water.

Porto Alegre seems to maintain a high standard of water governance. International sources have referred to it as an inspiring case study for every city attempting to improve its water governance. For example, the UK Local

112 With regards to the experience of users' engagement in water management and in particular of water users' associations see S. M. A. Salman, *The Legal Framework for Water Users' Associations: A Comparative Study*, World Bank Technical Paper no. 360 (Washington, D.C.: World Bank, 1997).

113 See 'National Participatory Approaches: Brazil', The Rights to Water and Sanitation, http://www.righttowater.info/rights-in-practice/rights-based-approach-for-practitioners/country-cases-of-participatory-approaches-to-legislation-and-policy-review/.

114 Brazil, Ley 10257/2001.

115 Brazil, Ley11445/2007.

116 Brazil, Ley 9433/1997.

Government Association deemed the process of Porto Alegre as 'an enormous success'.[117] The Association noted that 'women, ethnic minorities, low income and low education participants' are key participants in the funding decision-making process. Consequently, financial support for water improvements has been moved from the richest to the poorest parts of the city, which needed them to a greater extent. Accordingly, 'the power and influence of civil society' brought about a better allocation of resources and a system that is regarded as an outstanding example of participatory water governance.

Nonetheless, there has been criticism of some initiatives in Porto Alegre in the context of the Smart Cities Initiatives Framework.[118] The authors of one study commented on the success of Porto Alegre in terms of a city 'searching to be smarter'.[119] The authors analysed secondary data from official websites and other valid sources and combined this information with the factors of smart cities from the Chourabi et al.'s Framework. Although recognizing the inspiring role that Porto Alegre played for neighboring countries, the study underlined the presence of worrying social data and considerable income disparities. Despite the success of the participatory water management model, the city has not achieved those standards of social equality and income allocation that would qualify it as a 'smart city' under the Chourabi et al.'s Framework. Therefore, it can be concluded that even outstanding cases such as Porto Alegre still have improvements to make and lessons to learn.

ii *National Remedies and the Right to Water: The Case of the Matanza-Riachuelo River Basin, Argentina*

The Matanza-Riachuelo River Basin, in the metropolitan and industrial area of Buenos Aires, Argentina, not only is one of the most contaminated basins in Argentina, but is also characterized by high social and economic degradation. The river basin covers 2,240 km^2 and has a surrounding population of five million inhabitants. Around 368,000 m^3 of wastewater per day (derived from

117 Local Government Association, 'Case Study: Porto Alegre, Brazil', 12 December 2016, https://www.local.gov.uk/case-study-porto-alegre-brazil.

118 H. Chourabi, et al. 'Understanding Smart Cities: An Integrative Framework', *in Proceedings of the 45th Hawaii International Conference on System Sciences*, Maui, Hawaii, USA, 4–7 January 2012, pp. 2289–2297.

119 L. Schuch de Azambuja, et al. 'A Smart City Initiative: A Case Study of Porto Alegre', *in Proceedings of the 15th Annual International Conference on Digital Government Research*, Aguascalientes, Mexico, 18–21 June 2014 245–252.

sanitation services and industrial activities) are dumped into the river, and just 5% of this amount is properly treated.[120]

In 2004, a group of inhabitants of the river basin initiated a lawsuit before the Supreme Court of Argentina against the Argentinian state, the *Provincia de Buenos Aires*, the *Ciudad Autónoma de Buenos Aires*, and 44 enterprises, claiming social and environmental damages suffered by the group due to the pollution in the river. In 2006, a decision was issued by the Supreme Court, which urged the concerned authorities and enterprises to provide detailed information about the river basin's environmental condition.[121] The *Congreso Nacional* was responsive and five months later created the *Autoridad de la Cuenca Matanza-Riachuelo* (ACUMAR), an authority in charge of improving the environmental quality of the river water.

The final pronunciation of the Court was released in July 2008.[122] The Court's reasoning appears to be very pragmatic. Indeed, the Court defined an intervention plan which set out a series of measures to be implemented by ACUMAR. The Court stressed the need for public information, transparency in decision-making, civic involvement, constant monitoring by civil society, and periodic evaluations. The Court appointed a *Juzgado Federal* (Federal Court) of the area with the specific task of monitoring the implementation of these measures. In addition, the Court created a *Cuerpo Colegiado* (Collegial Body), coordinated by the *Defensor del Pueblo de la Nación* (National Ombudsman), with the aim of improving civic participation in monitoring.

The case is a remarkable example of a compromise among the state, businesses, and civil society achieved through the intervention of a judicial body. The Court did not expressly mention the RtW in its decision (it just dealt with the concept of the quality of life), but this does not undermine the value of the ruling. Rather than focusing on the RtW in abstract terms, the Court focused its decision on the issues to be solved and on how to practically resolve them. The RtW was instead mentioned by the NGOs standing in the case as third parties supporting the affected people. They focused their pleadings on the right to health, in which was inserted the RtW.[123]

Despite this promising 2008 ruling, the status quo seems to have been maintained. A recent article on the matter discloses the crude reality of

120 H.J. Franco & L. Armella, *La cuenca Matanza-RiachueLo: estado de situación de La sentencia de La Corte Suprema de Justicia de La nación en Los autos "Mendoza, Beatriz y otros c/ Estado Nacional"*, Instituto de Política Ambiental, 18 November 2010.

121 Argentina, Sentencia M. 1569.XL/2006, supra note 81.

122 Argentina, Sentencia M.1569.XL/2008.

123 Rulli & Justo, supra note 25, at 37.

Cuenca today.[124] Gutman cites the hearing on 30 November 2016 before the Supreme Court of Argentina in which Gabriela Seijo, Director of ACUMAR operations, publicly admitted that, up to that time, only 3,147 of the mandated 17,771 housing units—aimed at relocating those families most exposed to the pollution—had been provided. During the hearing, the Supreme Court Chief Justice, Ricardo Lorenzetti, an expert in ecology and a Goodwill Ambassador for Environmental Justice to the Organisation of American States, openly expressed his disappointment with the poor compliance record of ACUMAR. At the same hearing, Minister of Environment and Sustainable Development Sergio Bergman blamed the governments of Néstor Kirchner (2003–2007), president when ACUMAR was created, and Cristina Fernández de Kirchner (2007–2015), who held the presidency when the Court proclaimed the ruling of 2008, for the lack of progress. If the past presidents allegedly have not properly handled the issue, the current president, Mauricio Macri, in office since December 2015, has also faced criticism for not yet making substantial progress in forcing ACUMAR to respect the ruling.

On a positive note, 34,759 inspections of factories have been carried out and 57 plants consequently have closed. However, these figures are insignificant if one considers the fine million people living around the basin, of which at least ten per cent are in slums and shantytowns with poor access to water and in daily contact with contaminated river water.

iii *When the State Does Not Take into Account the Right to Water: The Case of Cochabamba, Bolivia*

A state that decides to orient its water system towards privatization must consider that the RtW restricts its options and asks to be balanced with the economic benefits of privatization. The case of the Bolivian city Cochabamba presents a good example of state decision-making that has failed to take this right into account.[125] The Cochabamba case is a clear example of privatization leading to the 'inevitable increases in tariffs that poor people cannot afford, and that, in turn, … threaten[s] the concept of the human right to water'.[126]

124 See D. Gutman, "The Riachuelo: A never-ending environmental disaster," *Buenos Aires Herald* (March 24, 2017), http://www.buenosairesherald.com/article/225083/the-riachuelo-a-neverending--environmental-disaster.

125 For more information about the case see also Salman & McInerney-Lankford, *supra* note 1, pp. 72–73; W. Finnegan, 'Letter from Bolivia—Leasing the Rain', *The New Yorker* (8 April 2002) at 43.

126 Salman & McInerney-Lankford, supra note 1, p. 72.

The area of Cochabamba was characterized by a public water management system from 1967 to 1999. The service was affected by inefficiencies (e.g., water loss) and low coverage of users. In 1997, only 57% of the inhabitants had direct access to water. The others had to buy it from private 'water vendors', often illegally and at a very high additional cost. In most of the city, the service functioned just one or two times per week.[127] The World Bank deemed an intervention necessary and offered to finance the service with a loan of US$25 million under the condition of the inclusion of private participation in the public water company.

The Bolivian government agreed to the condition and granted a private company, *Aguas del Tunari* (a consortium of foreign, including International Water Ltd., and Bolivian companies), a 40-year concession in 1999. Among the benefits entrusted to the enterprise were the full control of the water service, exclusive water rights, and an extra profit to remunerate the investment. For its part, the company committed itself (on paper) to grant quality service to the actual users, to expand the service to reach the inhabitants not yet connected to water service, and to guarantee accessibility, efficiency and equity in the provision of all its services. The private company was to be supervised by a governmental authority, the *Superintendencia*, which proved to be reluctant in the monitoring.

As often happens when a previously public service is affected by deficiencies, the *Aguas del Tunari* had to first improve the water infrastructure in order to widen coverage and improve efficiency. Predictably, their actions caused an average 43% increase in the tariff for the lower class and a 57% increase for the middle class, reaching the threshold of a 400% increase in some extreme cases.[128] These increases made the service unaffordable for a considerable part of the population and conflicted with the commitment of non-discrimination in the provision of water service. Moreover, the situation was worsened by the binding provisions of the contract concerning profit levels, the full recovery of investment costs, an unnecessary additional project envisaged by the contract (the Misicuni dam), and the calculation of the debt in foreign currency. Furthermore, the company, looking for additional profit, decided to take control of provision of water for 60 rural communities in the neighborhood of Cochabamba, threatening their ancestral link with nature (perceived as 'Mother Earth') and their already weak economy.[129]

---

127 Rulli & Justo, supra note 25, at 15.

128 Sjölander Holland, supra note 6, at 38–48.

129 Interview with Axel Dourojeanni, Experto Senior, Gerencia de Sutentabilidad, Fundación Chile, Santiago de Chile, 16 October 2014.

The state did not take any measures to re-equilibrate the service, for example, by providing subsidies. Consequently, a 'Water War' started: Demonstrations and violent actions affected the city, leading to the application of martial law, a circumstance that reminded the people of the atrocities suffered during the dictatorship (1971–1978). Trade unions, cooperatives of farmers, students, academics, and environmental organizations joined their efforts to create the *Coordinadora de Defensa del Agua y la Vida* (Organization for Water and Life Defense).

Due to these strong protests, in 2000, the *Superintendencia* decided to cancel the contract with the private company. This was seen as the first victory of the Bolivian people against the neoliberal model which had influenced the provision of public services during the previous fifteen years.[130] The main failure in the Bolivian state's decision to privatize water service can probably be found in the non-engagement of civil society in the decision-making process, either through consultation or the creation of panels for users' participation.

The decision was not quietly accepted by the private company and one of the partners of *Aguas del Tunari*, the enterprise Bechtel, initiated a lawsuit against the Bolivian government for US$25 billion before the International Centre for Settlement of Investment Disputes (ICSID), at the headquarters of the World Bank in Washington, D.C. The request by civil society groups to be represented before this forum or, at least, to attend the trial, was denied. An unbalanced panel was created for the decision. Three private judges were appointed to settle the dispute: an arbiter selected by Bechtel, one selected by the Bolivian government, and the president of ICSID, appointed by the World Bank (interestingly, it was the World Bank that urged the Bolivian government to privatize the service). It is evident that *de facto* in the panel two arbiters stood for the private investors, one for the state, and no one for civil society, the side most affected by the issue.

The ground-breaking nature of the Cochabamba case clearly emerges from current discussions on water conflicts. Particularly noteworthy are the reflections of Philippa DeBossier (Democracy Center, Cochabamba) writing 15 years after the Cochabamba victory.[131] The author points out that the lessons learnt from Cochabamba did not serve to stop conflicts between foreign corporations and local communities. Among these conflicts is that occurring in Peru

130 For a different and opposite opinion see Jampaglia & Molinari, supra note 90, at 132–133.

131 See P. de Boissière, 'Bolivia: 15 Years After the Cochabamba Water Revolt, Echos in New Cases of Corporate Abuse,' Upside Down World (28 April 2015), http://upsidedownworld.org/archives/bolivia/bolivia-15-years-after-the-cochabamba-water-revolt-echoes-in-new-cases-of-corporate-abuse/.

between the Spanish energy company Repsol and local indigenous communities, which threatens, among other natural elements, water in the fragile Amazonian ecosystems due to expansion of oil and gas exploitation. Again, in Peru, the Swiss commodities and mining conglomerate Glencore Xstrata is endangering the human right to water through the company's twin mega mining projects, Tintaya and Antapaccay, which menace the already scarce water supply. Finally, local communities and international organizations have engaged in actions over the Italo-Spanish energy multinational Enel-Endesa plans to flood 8,500 hectares of agricultural lands in Huila, Colombia in order to build a 400 MW dam to generate energy.

De Bossier elaborates on the worrying trend of conservative Latin America governments seeing foreign direct investment as a secure way to foster economic development. This may be true if the private investor develops a shared agenda of operations together with the local government and the interested community and takes into account the imperative of minimizing environmental externalities. Without this shared commitment, the state risks 'giving away' a country's precious resources without securing an adequate economic return. Moreover, even a satisfactory economic return is not sufficient to compensate for the unrepairable loss of environmental richness and the violation of the human right to water.

Although these dynamics are similar to the Cochabamba case, the situation is exacerbated by the climate crisis and this should make governments even more cautious when giving away natural resources. Irresponsible resource exploitation not only threatens the RtW of the affected communities, but also increases their climate vulnerability and resilience. In her concluding words, De Bossier calls for international solidarity as happened in Cochabamba, this time in support of the resistance movements in Peru and Colombia against climate change driving multinationals. These case studies in Bolivia, Peru and Colombia show that a constructive dialogue and a cooperative attitude based on the mutual compromise is the only way forward, both for the affected communities, for the contracting states, and for the companies involved in water governance.

B The Main Features of Public, Private, and Mixed Water Systems in Latin America

I *Models for Water Management*

The discussion on the possible conflict between the RtW and privatization continues with an analysis of the RtW in the context of both public and private water management models. The main features of market and public services are investigated in order to understand the actual meaning of 'privatization' of the water system. The concept of privatization will be subsequently discussed in detail in Part C on the Chilean scenario.

a From Public Management to Different Degrees of Private Intervention

The *governance of water supply* is a key topic in the debate on water. The term 'refers to the range of political, social, economic and administrative systems that are in place to develop and *manage* water resources, and the delivery of water services, at different levels of society'.[132] The concept of governance is broader than management because the former includes the latter, and governance refers to the broader social system of governing water-related topics, which means even (but not only) the government decision-making process on water.[133] However, the two concepts are intrinsically linked.[134]

As affirmed before, water differs from other resources because of the restrictions linked to its nature. First, the water market *per se* is not a competitive market but a natural monopoly. This implies, for natural reasons (the indispensability of water, its very nature as a scarce resource), that unlimited entry into the sector to expand water supply is almost impossible. Those firms charged with its provision will generally remain the sole providers in the market. This outcome also derives from reasons linked to the economies of scale: the cost of construction of a competitive set of water and sewerage pipes in a city would prove to be higher than the profit from the parallel supply.[135] Therefore, the possible options for water management represent just a second best, a suboptimal solution, economically speaking, given that the optimum cannot be achieved due to the particularities of the sector.

Secondly, the water system needs a considerable amount of resources, which have to be obtained while maintaining the financial balance of the provider. The need for significant investment has stimulated states to open the market to private actors but, in order to make them interested in financing

---

132 Global Water Partnership, *Introducing Effective Water Governance*, mimeo, April 2002.

133 See also P. Rogers & A. W. Hall, *Effective Water Governance*, Global Water Partnership Technical Committee, Background Paper no. 7 (Stockholm: Global Water Partnership, 2003).

134 See 'Water Management & Governance', IHE Delft, https://www.un-ihe.org/water-management-governance-0.

135 See 'Natural monopoly,' from Economics Online, http://www.economicsonline.co.uk/Business_economics/Natural_monopolies.html.

the sector, the conditions of participation would have to be attractive for the company. The risks cannot fall just on the private supplier. Further, the framework for participation cannot be too strict, but must be flexible to deal with eventual mutations of market conditions. At the same time, the state's decision to entrust the private company must consider the limits explained above that correspond to the content of the RtW.

At a theoretical level, three models for water management can be identified, but it is very unlikely to come across one of them in its 'pure' version: more often one finds halfway solutions that present characteristics of more than one model. The three main models will be described as a useful starting point to reflect on their advantages and disadvantages. Massarutto[136] schematized them as follows:

- Under *direct public management* the public body is entrusted with the provision of water services, the control is hierarchical, and the applicable law is public law. There is no competition but there can be a tender for the procurement and some forms of outsourcing. The threat of privatization is the main incentive to the good governance of the system.
- The *delegated management* (in its pure form, all the managerial activities involving the supply of water are delegated) to a private entity through a concession for a set period of time. The remuneration of the private company derives from the right to collect a tariff. The company is chosen through a competitive public tender, i.e. the best offer will obtain the concession and a contract will regulate it. There is no competition *in* the market but competition *for* the market. The main threat is the republicizing of the sector. A variant of this hypothesis is the concession not only of the management, but also of the ownership of the water supply network, a circumstance which increases the engagement of the private partner.
- If the private supplier is not chosen by a competitive public tender, or the winning bid is not the best offer, or the concession period is very long or even indefinite, or the conditions to withdraw the concession are excessively onerous for the state, then the second model makes a shift to a third model, the *regulated private monopoly*. The regulation of the management is discretional, based on a set of rules (water provision standards, maximum tariff, conditions of access) issued by the public authority, but there is no contract. Some mechanisms are implemented to avoid the risk of monopoly revenues. Indeed, lacking competition, the state undertakes measures to incentivize the efficiency of the provider based on remuneration (for

136 Massarutto, supra note 90, at 105–115.

example, the mechanism of a price cap)[137] and yardstick competition (i.e., the constant comparison among different possibilities of management)[138] in order to simulate the functioning of a truly competitive market.

Halfway solutions are, for example, schemes of risk sharing like the public-private partnership (PPP), the network's lease contracts (the so-called "affermage" contract),[139] and user cooperatives.

b The Concepts of Market Service and Public Service

Massarutto sets out the distinction between the concepts of 'market service' (MS) and 'public service' (PS).[140] Under the MS scenario, the provider is free to set the price, the features of the service offered (quality, technical, and commercial requisites), and where to allocate it. Under the PS scenario, those elements are fixed by the public authority (or, at least, approved by it) and the citizen has the right to demand that the state ensures the provider is in compliance with them. Moreover, in a MS setting the consumer is free to negotiate with the provider and to agree with its conditions of supply; the same freedom belongs to the provider, which can choose whether they want to bargain with the potential user. In contrast, in a PS setting, it is the public authority that has the duty to negotiate with each user, but it can also oblige the user to sign a contract. In the MS setting, the supplier is free to withdraw the contract, possibly paying a penalty, whereas in the PS setting the public authority establishes the causes leading to the interruption of the contract's execution. Furthermore, in the MS setting the economic risk falls on the private operator, while in the PS setting it falls partially on the public body.

Further, in the MS setting the general principles on competition cannot be derogated (in Europe these principles are enshrined in the Treaty on the

137 See 'Features of the Price Cap and Revenue Cap Regulation', Body of Knowledge on Infrastructure Regulation, http://regulationbodyofknowledge.org/price-level-regulation/features-of-price-cap-and-revenue-cap-regulation/.

138 See Netherlands Bureau for Economic Policy Analysis, *Yardstick Competition: Theory, Design and Practice*, Working Paper No. 133, (The Hague, 2000), http://www.cpb.nl/en/publication/yardstick-competition-theory-design-and-practice.

139 The 'affermage' contract is a 'type of lease where the owner of assets leases them to a private operator, who takes on the full managerial and commercial risk. Investment planning, financing and execution rest with the owner. The operator should be responsible for all maintenance and investment at the production centers'. Definition by the Lagos Water Corporation available at http://www.lagoswater.org/lwc_psp_mini_site/psp_tipbits.htm.

140 Massarutto, supra note 90, at 98–99.

Functioning of the European Union).[141] In the PS setting it is possible to disregard them in order to make the obligation of fair and equal provision sustainable. Yet, in the MS setting in cases of the user's non-fulfillment of the obligation to pay, the sanctions are foreseen by the contract and by the civil code, including the suspension of the provision of water. In contrast, in the PS setting, these consequences are regulated by the contract with the public entity, which may exclude such a suspension. Finally, MS litigations are decided before a civil judge; in the PS, disputes are settled by the public authority.

c The Real Meaning of the Concept of 'Privatization'

At this stage, it is necessary to analyze the content of the concept of 'privatization' because a misleading debate has developed based on the wrong assumption that *any* form of private participation in the sector implies privatization. The ideological impact of the concept is one of the factors that has caused the demagogy and lack of pragmatism characteristic of the water debate. In reality, very few water systems are completely privatized and without any regulation derived from a public authority. The lack of any regulation from the public authority on a water system should be properly called privatization, while in the majority of the cases it is just identified as '*participation* of the private sector'.

The following models present an increasing scale of private intervention.[142] First, the lowest form of private participation is a service contract granted by a public authority through which a private entrepreneur is charged with managing the water system. In the second model the contract is the same but with a private company, concerning the leasing of the infrastructure to the private actor. In the third model fall limited time leases related to the water network for the creation or renewal of infrastructures (the BOOT model, 'build-own-operate-transfer')[143] and the concession of the service management to a private firm which commits itself to respect the terms of the concession contract (the most common option). Finally, the most radical option is the partial or total sale of the rights and the infrastructure of the water network to a private company.

The analysis can be refined and further summarized by considering the presence or absence of public control. As regarding the most common of

---

141 Consolidated Version of the Functioning of the European Union, 2008 OJ C115/47 (TFEU), arts. 101(1)–(3), 102, 106, 107.

142 Segerfeldt, supra note 90, at 84.

143 For further information on the BOOT Model see: http://www.businessdictionary.com/definition/build-own-operate-transfer-BOOT.html.

the water management models discussed above, state control can be identified in all of them. As regards the direct public management, state control is obvious; in the delegated management model, it happens through the terms of the concession contract and, even in the case of the natural monopoly, the state can be present through price or performance regulations. Therefore, the instances in which the intervention of the state is nearly absent are very rare,[144] one of which is Chile. Nonetheless, private providers will have to be aware of the strategic importance of water as a public service, even when the state has a limited role in managing the sector. Indeed, such respect will help the water provider in understanding people's needs, public concerns, and, most important, it may prove to be preferable in terms of cost-effectiveness.

One of the basic principles that should orient water governance is the right to water access for each individual and equity in this access. In countries with a significant proportion of the population living in poverty, this portion of the population represents a significant water demand, which the private operator cannot ignore if it does not want to lose a section of consumers. Numerous studies demonstrated that the developing countries where the private companies have invested in the water system show a level of access to water higher than in countries where this intervention is lacking.[145]

Generally, the main factor that makes a private firm willing to invest in the sector is the opportunity to make a profit. The question (already partially addressed in Part A) is whether the profit is in conflict with the principles that should guide the sector. In order to answer this question, it should be considered that profit has three components: the pure cost of the invested capital (this element should not be contested), the incentive price to the investor (as a necessary stimulant for the investor to improve the efficiency of the system) and the extra-profit deriving from the monopoly (eventual and dependant on the role of the provider in the market). Only this last component should be at issue because it does not reward the efficiency of the provider, but derives from the exploitation of a particular position performed on a market characterized by a 'rigid' request. Indeed, in a market such as the essential utilities' market, an increase of price does not alter the quantity demanded by users. Therefore, the provider can augment the tariff without worrying about diminution of its request.[146]

144 Segerfeldt, supra note 90, at 85.

145 Ibid., at 86.

146 Massarutto, supra note 90, at 132–138.

d Comparison of the Water Management Framework in Latin America and Europe

In order to provide an overview of the water network management in the area of interest, Latin America, it is useful to reflect on the factors that affect the LA scenario, based on the data collected by Dourojeanni,[147] as compared with the factors characterizing the European scenario, pursuant to the analysis of Vergès.[148] This comparison will facilitate the understanding of certain features that are peculiar to LA's water systems.

Four main factors substantially differentiate these two areas.[149] Each of these factors is examined in turn below, namely, the geographic and demographic context, the level of socioeconomic development, the territorial framework for water governance, and the economic regulation of the water sector.

First, with regard to the *geographic and demographic context*, in general, the European countries are a limited geographic area and have a high geographical concentration of inhabitants. A situation of water abundance is predominant, excluding someareas in Spain, Italy and Greece. In contrast, in Latin America, in general, countries have a broad geographic area, a low geographic concentration of inhabitants (i.e. long distances between inhabited areas), and difficult terrain. While Latin America encompasses many different scenarios, in general, a situation of water scarcity is registered in many countries.

The *level of socioeconomic development* in Latin America and Europe varies widely in each region and can only be described in general terms here. For example, the level of socioeconomic development within Europe is quite different between Eastern European states (less developed)[150] and Western European (more developed). Nevertheless, the GDP per capita of member states of the European Union, the purchasing power being equal, is four times higher than the average of GDP per capita in Latin America.

The principles of equality in access to water and the grant of a certain quality of water to everyone are definitely better implemented in Europe than in Latin America (despite the lack of insertion of the RtW in constitutions). In general, the proportion of defaulting users in Europe is low (on average

---

147 A. C. Dourojeanni, *Thematic Study on the Common Problems and Challenges in the Integrated Management of Water Resources and Coasts in the Context of Climate Change in Latin America*, EuropeAid/129783/C/SER/multi, Specific contract No. 2012/298550, Version 1 (2012b).

148 Vergès, supra note 97.

149 Ibid., at 9–11.

150 It should be noted that in Eastern Europe the issues and weaknesses of the water sector have been considerably reduced due to actions by the EU.

1 or 2%, and even lower in France, e.g., 0.6 %), while they represent an important concern in Latin America (reaching more than half the inhabitants for the poorest states such as Peru).

The debate on water in each of these two areas highlights different concerns. In Europe, the main issues are related to water pollution and to the high costs for treatment of water deriving from sanitation. In Latin America, the main issues are related to the need of expanding water access under fair economic conditions, providing sanitation service for all, and dealing with the consequences of drought more than with environmental concerns. These circumstances affect the water sector, shaping its features differently. This implies a different allocation of resources to resolve them. In Europe, resources will be focussed on improving the environmental sustainability of the water sector; in Latin America, resources will be focussed on eliminating social and territorial inequalities, improving water quality, and expanding water coverage in rural and suburban areas.

The *territorial framework for water governance* is very different in the two areas and within each area itself. In Europe, there is high territorial fragmentation of the sub-national institutions involved in water resources management (for example, numerous municipalities are charged with water governance in Italy, Germany, and France), however, low fragmentation with a tendency to centralization of institutions is shown in England.

In Latin America, a variety of solutions are registered: in some areas there is a high number of institutions involved in water resources management, which often results in inefficiencies. This is because effective mechanisms are rarely implemented to facilitate integration of the respective strategies or to predict the impacts that their combined actions may have on the environment.[151] This occurs in numerous municipalities in Colombia, Mexico, and Brazil. In contrast, a low fragmentation is registered in Chile. As a consequence, in those states characterized by fragmentation, municipalities have autonomy in the governance of the water service,[152] whereas the centralization leads to a low level of autonomy for the municipality.

The institutional framework of the state in these two regions is very diverse as well. For example, Germany (with its federal organization through '*länder*') and Italy (not a federal state, but with its '*regioni*' granted with legislative and fiscal autonomy) are characterized by decentralization, while England has a

151 Dourojeanni, supra note 147, at 114.

152 In Italy, the municipalities' autonomy was high before the *Legge Galli* (the 1994 Law establishing an Integrated Urban Water Management for Italy) but was consistently reduced because of the intervention of this law.

strongly centralized institutional framework. France, despite its territorial fragmentation of water management, does not present either federal or strong decentralization because its regions lack both legislative and fiscal autonomy. Similarly, in Latin America, high institutional decentralization is registered in Brazil and Mexico, while centralization characterizes the institutions in Chile (likely due to its particular geography) and, finally, Colombia presents a form of 'de-concentration' (but not yet decentralization) in regions with very little autonomy, similar to France.

Governance of the water sector also varies depending upon the type of economic regulation to which the provider is subjected. There is not a unique orientation characterizing each area; instead various assets may be identified. A national independent authority governs the sector in England, Colombia, and Chile.[153] In France, Germany, Scandinavia, Italy, and Mexico, there is no similar authority but regulation is contained in concessions contracts, which delegate the service to a specific company. Finally, national regulation that is limited to a public system of information collection and to forms of benchmarking[154] characterizes the water systems in the Netherlands and Brazil, but for the latter state, the adoption of Ley Federal No. 11.445/2007 has modified the scenario.

For the overall framework, it is necessary to point out that, in spite of the aforementioned dissimilarities, some common lines of development can be identified when analyzing the matter in a future-oriented perspective. First, the presence of the private actor in the water sector is growing. Second, there is a rising demand for civic engagement. Third, there is increasing concern for the environment and for the efficient treatment of water derived from sanitation services.

From this last point it can be seen that there is growing awareness that fragmentation is not an efficient way to solve these issues and the need for an integrated system of water resource management has to be acknowledged. Furthermore, a tendency can be identified towards the separation of the service's administration (involving politicians) from its provision (involving

---

153 For the Chilean case see the particularities of its system, namely the weaknesses of the *Dirección General de Aguas*.

154 Benchmarking is, following the definition of the American Water Works Association, 'a systematic process of searching for best practices, innovative ideas, and highly effective operating procedures that lead to superior performance and then adapting those practices, ideas, and procedures to improve the performance of one's own organization'. See also R. Parena & E. Smeets, 'Benchmarking Initiatives in the Water Industry', *Water Science and Technology*, Vol. 44(2–3) (2001), pp. 103–110.

technicians). Indeed, the first is in the hands of institutional bodies, while the latter is in the hands of specialized companies.

Yet, the need for an autonomous entity responsible for economic regulation and monitoring of the operator, in order to depoliticize the sector, is urgent. Finally, the need of implementing of benchmarking methods must be underlined. As a result of the high complexity of these needs, a deeper analysis of the water management systems in the two regions is materially impossible in this context. However, an overview on the main tendencies registered within the sector will follow.

In Latin America, a diverse set of solutions for water management can be identified. Imagining a litmus paper test of the level of private intervention in the sector, the set goes from highly and strongly privatized water sectors to contexts in which privatization is firmly prohibited even through constitutional statements. A few examples are mentioned here to convey this idea of variety:

- *The privatization at its highest level of implementation*: the Chilean water and sanitation services.
- *The intermediate solution*, i.e. both the models are allowed: the Mexican and Peruvian water and sanitation services.
- *The ban on privatization by law or inserted in constitution*: the Uruguayan and Ecuadorean water and sanitation services (for the specific legal provisions see Part A above).

In spite of this multifaceted scenario, it must be underlined that the majority of LA governments have agreed, mostly through incorporation in their most recent water legislation (see Part A above), but in some cases just at a theoretical level, on some common principles, that have been inspired by the international debate on water. Among those common objectives, remarkably there is the commitment to a system of water management based on environmental needs and sensitivity to the issue of climate change, as well as incentives towards integrated water resource management and the calculation, compensation, and reduction of corporations' water footprint.[155]

The data collected[156] in Latin America demonstrates that in the region, all the countries present at least two levels of water authorities: at the national and regional levels. At the national level, the water authority is strictly linked

155 P. Schulte, *Corporate Water Disclosure Guidelines. Toward a Common Approach to Reporting Water Issues* (Oakland, CA: Pacific Institute, CEO Water Mandate, 2014).

156 Dourojeanni, supra note 147.

to the Ministry of Environment (in Mexico and Brazil), the Ministry of Water and Environment (in Bolivia), the Ministry of Agriculture (in Peru), and the Ministry of Public Works (in Chile).

Further, in those countries with indigenous peoples, including Panama, Ecuador, Peru, Chile and Bolivia, local communities often have gained forms of water resources management attentive to their traditions and of the special link they have with Mother Earth.

Often, this 'traditional' management is flanked by modern systems of agriculture, mining exploitation, and industry. These two ways of management do not always run in parallel without impinging one upon another. As a matter of fact, conflicts frequently arise between the interests of the indigenous populations and those of private (often foreign) corporations, which intervene in the territory of the indigenous peoples and disregard the ancient values that used to orient their way of living. Chilean case law contains several examples, including the case concerning the Pascua-Lama mining project and its impact on the Huasco Valley.

Another important element to consider is continuity in water policies. First, a good continuity in water policies and governance in the hands of competent technicians is identified in Brazil, mainly due to the efficiency of the National Water Agency, and in Chile, where the private sector is stable and owns a consistent amount of resources to be invested in research. Moreover, some public-private foundations are active in the field of innovation for water management, like the Fundación Chile.[157]

Second, an unstable history of water policies characterizes, for example, Peru although attempts to stabilize it are in place. Often in such countries, international agreements have played an important role in stabilizing the sector, imposing or suggesting guidelines for action to the government.

Generally speaking, the following deficits can be pointed out in water governance in Latin America.[158] First, there is a lack of 'culture of compliance' (*cultura de pago*). There is misunderstanding on how the concept of the RtW is interpreted by people: dominates a belief in the intrinsic nature of the right, considering to be a right indispensable to life and a good that people do not have to pay for. Secondly, there is no priority given to assigning financial resources to a river basin in order to properly govern it. Thirdly, the increase of interventions in a river basin is made without scaling up the capabilities of management of such interventions. Urban areas often are affected by a deficit

157 Fundación Chile—Agua & Medio Ambiente, see http://www.fch.cl/sustentabilidad.

158 A. C. Dourojeanni, *La Gestión del Agua en los Límites de Disponibilidad en Latinoamérica* (Santiago: Gerencia de Agua & Medio Ambiente, Fundación Chile, 2012a) at 52–60.

in watershed management, and do not include river restoration in their political plans.

Furthermore, private companies are only now starting to reflect on environmental concerns, sustainability, and resource preservation from a long-term perspective. In addition, the mining sector, where active, is entitled with excessive powers and rarely compromises on social and environmental needs. The agriculture sector, for its part, constantly claims for an increase in hydraulic infrastructure, ignoring the concerns of water scarcity. In particular, in desert areas, groundwater aquifers have been destroyed due to the intensive extraction of water for irrigation, mining, and industrial use. In general, a widespread lack of integrated water management affects the Latin American region, where a narrow and short minded vision is dominant.

As for private involvement in the European context, this 'profitable market' is experiencing a growing expansion of the private sector, as noted by the powerful water company Suez in its 2003 Report on Future Goals.[159] Two of the markets considered the most interesting in the Report are Italy and Germany. Suez believes that the growing pressure as a result of of the European Union's high environmental standards, as well as states' financial concerns, will encourage EU governments towards privatization. Indeed, the implementation of EU regulations is often very expensive and demands technical competence, and therefore resources, that the state often lacks, whereas such competencies are usually owned by private firms. The potential of the market is considerable because 70% of European water services are still in public hands.[160] Moreover, the costs of the initial investment required in Europe are lower than in LA countries because the majority of European countries already have good water and sanitation infrastructure. Indeed, Latin America is now facing the issue (namely, the lack of adequate water and sanitation infrastructure), that Europe solved in the middle of the nineteenth century.

The solutions adopted in Europe for water management can be divided into three groups, as in Latin America:

- *Privatized water management*, with water infrastructure sold to private firms, is only found in England and Wales (high implemented privatization, but not liberalization of the market).
- *Lack of any form of private involvement*, as in Luxembourg, The Netherlands, Sweden, and Finland. These countries have prohibited the shift to privatization through various legal tools. Among the Eastern Europe countries, Poland still has a public form of management.

159 Sjölander Holland, supra note 6, at 223.

160 Ibid., at 228.

- A form of *private participation inserted in the public management system* through different instruments like concession contracts, public-private partnerships, or leasing of infrastructure is the most common scenario in the majority of the Western European states not mentioned above, particularly Italy, Germany, Austria, and Spain. Among Eastern European states, a shift to private participation has been led by Croatia, Albania, the Czech Republic, Macedonia, Uzbekistan, and Tajikistan, under incentives offered by the World Bank.[161]

In general, the following common features of the European water sector can be underlined. There is a growing shift to (partial) privatization of water and sanitation services, the reasons for a state to privatize being often similar, for example, municipal financial concerns. The involvement of the private sector is also related to the growing necessity for investment and technical knowledge, mainly to comply with EU standards. This also results in the creation of autonomous water supply companies controlled by municipalities (but with an asset similar to private companies).

It should be added that the private intervention rarely has been conducted without civic complaints. One of the main reasons for these complaints is that the private participation has often caused an increase in the tariff. In general, water tariffs are related to consumption and not to the individual financial situation of consumers. Therefore, 'substantial' equality in the access to water is not always achieved.

Furthermore, the mechanism of full cost recovery,[162] as affirmed at Article 9 of in the EU's Water Framework Directive,[163] strongly affects water tariffs and a users' claim for a tariff reduction. It is true that the cost of water is only a small part of the budget of most Europeans, and such costs can be an incentive to

161 S. Mohajeri, B. Knothe, D-N. Lamothe & J-A. Faby (eds.), *European Water Management between Regulation and Competition* (Luxembourg: Office for Official Publications of the European Communities, 2003).

162 '[Full] cost recovery' can be defined as 'the [total] recuperation of the costs of government-provided or funded products, services or activities that, at least in part, provide private benefits to individuals, entities or groups, or reflect the costs their actions impose'. *Cost Recovery Guidelines*, Department of Treasury and Finance, State Government Victoria, Australia (2013) at 5.

163 Directive 2000/60/EC of the European Parliament and of the Council establishing a framework for the Community action in the field of water policy, OJ L 327, 22 December 2000 [Water Framework Directive], art. 9: 'Member States shall take account of the principle of recovery of the costs of water services, including environmental and resource costs, having regard to the economic analysis conducted according to Annex III, and in accordance in particular with the polluter pays principle'.

reduce one's use of water. Nevertheless, for low-income households the tariff can represent a burden, being up to five percent of their annual budget as assessed by the Transnational Institute and Corporate Europe Observatory.[164]

Notwithstanding, the commitment to achieve universality in water service is often strong and effectively met. It is also remarkable that the qualitative aspects of drinking water and sewage services receive high and constant attention. In addition, it is noteworthy that the necessity of sustainable and environmentally respectful water management is generally acknowledged. The public water systems of Vienna, Munich, and Amsterdam are particularly efficient in this regard.

Comparing the frameworks for water management in Europe and Latin America, the main similarities are as follows:

- Growing presence of the private element.
- Constant demand for tariff reduction.
- Growing need for more detailed technical information and managerial skills.
- Increasing number of requests for civic engagement in water-related decisions.

In general, the main differences are as follows:

- In Latin America, the water scenario is characterized by the predominance of water scarcity, a culture of non-payment, and the uncertainty of water companies' profit, which does not give them the incentive to make investments in the water sector.
- The European water sector is considered a stable and profitable market and private companies in general aim to expand it. The abundance of water and the tendency for users to comply with the obligation to pay the water bill are other favorable factors for private investors.

In Latin America, a general level of abstraction can be identified in the debate on the water sector with constitutional and legal statements against privatization on one side, and, on the other side, a deficit of concrete implementation of them and lack of compliance with rules. However, there are some exceptions, i.e. the implementation of tangible solutions and concrete improvements.

---

164 D. Hachfeld P. Terhorst, and O. Hoedeman, *Progressive Public Water Management in Europe. In search of exemplary cases* (The Transnational Institute and Corporate Europe Observatory, 2009) at 13–14.

Generally, in Europe, the approach to water issues is more practical, likely aimed to offset the (dominant) lack of legal recognition of the public management of the system. There is a tendency to develop realistic compromise solutions between public and private interests. Contrary to what is registered in Latin America, in Europe there is certainly more compliance with norms. Moreover, in Latin America, official regulations for water management operators are often scarce and addressed to only a few operators, while in Europe, the water sector is characterized by a high level of regulations, addressed generally to all the operators in the sector. It is noteworthy that in Latin America there is a certain deficit in clarity of the institutional roles of the actors operating in the water sector, and there are few protocols for water management and non-compliance with them. European water institutions' roles are more clearly defined, due to the numerous protocols on water management and to general compliance with them. Finally, it should be added that an important concern of the LA scenario is the lack of adequate financing for innovative initiatives, while in the Europe, in general, innovative initiatives are financed, although not yet sufficiently.

e The Contribution of the EU to Latin America's Water Resource Management

The European context on water resource management has been deeply influenced by the presence of the European Union. Three main lines of action have shaped the European debate on water privatization:

- The development of new social rights in EU legislation, among which are some forms of (indirect) recognition of the RtW (see also Part A).
- The imposition of certain environmental standards on domestic legislators under EU legislation.
- The principles elaborated by the EU for the creation of the common market[165] and the implementation of balanced, and transparent rules on competition[166] with which national states have to comply.

---

165 The creation of a common market was the main aim of the Treaty establishing the European Economic Community, signed in Rome in 1957, which at Article 2 affirms that 'the Community shall have as its task, by establishing a common market and progressively approximating the economic policies of Member States, to promote throughout the Community a harmonious development of economic activities …'. Further, Article 26(2) of the TFEU (Part 3, Title I), supra note 140, states that 'the internal market shall comprise an area without internal frontiers in which the free movement of goods, persons, services and capital is ensured …'.

166 TFEU, ibid., Part 3, Title VII, Chapter 1, Rules on competition. In particular, TFEU, arts. 101(1), 101(2)&(3), 102, 106, 107.

As regards the first two points, the Charter of Fundamental Rights of the European Union has indirectly granted the RtW through Article 2 of (on the right to life), Article 35 (on the protection of the human health), Article 36 (on the access to services of general economic interest), Article 37 (on environmental protection and sustainable development), and Article 38 (on consumers' protection).[167]

Therefore, the EU has a dual approach to water: on one hand, it recognizes the particular and fragile nature of the resource which must be preserved, but on the other hand, it inserts the water utility in the framework of services of general interests. These interests have to be managed with respect to the national financial budget and to the leading principles on competition, despite the possibility of balancing them according to the specialty of the service and with respect to the principle of institutional autonomy.

In relation to the third point listed above, namely the creation of the common market, it is noteworthy that this has played a crucial role in determining the shift towards water service privatization. Among the other directives on the topic, Directive 2004/17/CE is particularly relevant issued by the European Parliament jointly with the Council on 31 March 2004.[168] It coordinates the procurement procedures of entities operating in the water, energy, transport and postal services sectors.

The position of the EU with regards to the involvement of the private operator in the water sector has been controversial. On one side, the European Commission has demonstrated that it is in favor of improving the internal market through the participation of the private sector. Two papers which have strongly incentivized this are the Internal Market Strategy Priorities 2003–2006[169] and the Guidelines for Successful Public-Private Partnership of 2003.[170] The PPP is presented as the most desirable solution to water management. On the other side, the European Parliament has generally opposed water privatization, considering water as a good not suitable to market rules. Nevertheless, the situation is different for initiatives with non-EU countries, where both institutions agree on the need to create favorable conditions for

167 Charter of Fundamental Rights, supra note 61.

168 Directive 2004/17/EC of the European Parliament and of the Council of 31 March 2004 coordinating the procurement of entities operating in the water, energy, transport, and postal service sectors, OJ L 134/1, 30 April 2004.

169 Text available at http://ec.europa.eu/internal_market/strategy/previous_strategy_en.htm.

170 European Commission, Directorate-General Regional Policy, *Guidelines for Successful Public-Private Partnerships*, (March 2003), http://eur-lex.europa.eu/legal-content/EN/TXT/HTML/?uri=CELEX:52003DC0238&from=EN.

private intervention. Two bodies have been created for this purpose: namely, the EU Water Initiative and the EU Water Fund.[171]

Nothing similar to the EU can be found in Latin America. The countries in this region, because of their different historical, social, and economic development, have not achieved any kind of integration comparable to that realized by the European Union. Nonetheless, some attempts towards integration have occurred. Notably, the proposal of the Andean Community (*Comunidad Andina*), an organization founded under the 1969 Cartagena Agreement, gathered a number of LA countries together with the aim of joint integrated development on a voluntary basis. Currently, the *Comunidad* parties are Bolivia, Colombia, Ecuador, and Peru. Chile was a member of the organization until 1976, when Pinochet decided to withdraw Chile from the accord due to the economic incompatibilities of the pact with the state's aims. Venezuela was also a party between 1973 and 1976. The party states share a common history, a patchy geography, and a multiform cultural, ethnic, and linguistic society. The *Comunidad* is organized through bodies and institutions that form the Andean Ingegration System (*Sistema Andino de Integración*).[172]

In the water field, in particular, the *Comunidad* issued the *Estrategia Andina para la Gestión Integrada de los Recursos Hídricos* in 2011.[173] The aim of the Strategy was to implement a directive for common regulation of water resource management among the member states with the possibility of extending it to other countries. The *Comunidad* has not succeeded in this regard, but the idea and the efforts made to achieve it are commendable.

It is also worthwhile mentioning the Community of Latin American and Caribbean States (*Comunidad de Estados Latinoamericanos y Caribeños*—CELAC), an intergovernmental organization, created under the Caracas Declaration. It regroups the heads of state and government of Latin American and Caribbean states and represents a step towards a higher cooperation level and towards cultural and political integration in the region. From the market perspective, the older *Sistema Económico Latinoamericano y del Caribe* (SELA)[174] can also be mentioned. It was created by the Panama Convention, which has sought to enhance economic integration in the region, although not at a level comparable to the former European Communities.

171 Sjölander Holland, supra note 6, at 223–227.

172 See http://www.comunidadandina.org/.

173 Decisión 763, Estrategia Andina para la Gestión Integrada de los Recursos Hídricos, vigésimo tercera Reunión Ordinaria del Consejo Andino de Ministros de Relaciones Exteriores, Lima, Peru, 22 August 2011.

174 See http://www.sela.org.

Despite the absence of an EU counterpart in Latin America, the EU has developed forms of cooperation within the region and has relations with supranational bodies such as the CELAC. The EU's influence in Latin America has been implemented through a set of important steps, recently involving the CELAC. First, a June 1999 meeting in Rio de Janeiro instituted a partnership among Latin America, the Caribbean, and the EU. The summit held in Santiago de Chile in 2013 represented the first official meeting between the EU and the CELAC[175] and dealt with, among other topics, bi-regional cooperation on the environment, sustainable development, and climate change.[176] A new summit between the EU and the CELAC was held in Brussels in 2015 under the theme: "Shaping our common future: working for prosperous, cohesive and sustainable societies for our citizens".

The EU has contributed to the Latin America's water sector at a technical level through the implementation of the principles stated in the framework of the aforementioned summits. The support has focused, among other topics, on the sustainability of water management in urban areas, dealing with drought and the prevention of natural disasters such as floods, the enhancement of water quality and sanitation services, the improvement of wastewater treatment, balancing environmental concerns with claims for a higher use of water from agriculture, industry, mining, and energy production. Following Dourojeanni,[177] tangible actions have been implemented, including financing mechanisms essential to improving water governance, studies and analysis to achieve efficient river basin management, support to local governments with a particular interest at the municipal level in order to improve managerial skills and, specifically, to build an integrated water resource management system. In particular the European Commission financed the Latin American Network of Knowledge Centers in the Water Sector (RALCEA) Project, with a contribution of €2.25 million between 2010 and 2015.[178] The project, implemented in Latin America and Cuba, aimed at improving the water sector by addressing one of the principal issues facing this sector, namely the lack of adequate technical knowledge based on joint research and advanced studies. Several EU member states, namely, Germany, the Netherlands, Italy, France, Spain, and Belgium,

175 For more information on relations between the EU and the CELAC see http://www.eeas.europa.eu.

176 See European Parliament, 'America Latina e Caraibi' (2017), http://www.europarl.europa.eu/RegData/etudes/fiches_techniques/2013/060602/04A_FT(2013)060602_IT.pdf.

177 Further information available at Dourojeanni, supra note 146 at 13–15.

178 See World Water Forum, Solutions for Water Platform, 'Latin American Network of Knowledge Centres in the Water Sector (RALCEA Project)', http://www.solutionsforwater.org/wp-content/uploads/2012/03/RALCEA_Fiche_Project.pdf.

plus Switzerland and the United States have provided bilateral assistance to LA states, as part of RALCEA.[179]

f Examples of Efficient Public Water Management

Several examples of efficient public water management (PbWM) are noteworthy:

- The public water management system of Porto Alegre, Brazil (see Part A above) is characterized by a strong civic engagement in the decision-making process through mechanisms of direct democracy, a high level of transparency, excellent water quality, water service cost that is one of the lowest in Latin America, water access by 99.5 % of the population (very surprising data, considering the average value registered in Latin America on this topic), and sanitation service covering 84% of the population.[180]
- The Colombian public company of Medellin, EPM, is active in energy supply, natural gas and water provision, and proves to be extremely efficient, not only in water supply, but in developing a sustainable approach to river basin management.[181]
- The Ecuadorean public company, ETAPA, with its multisector scope of action, is another great example of an efficient public management system.[182]
- The cooperative of Santa Cruz, Bolivia, Saguapac, is recognized as one of the best-run public water companies. The access percentage is considerably high and so is the percentage of paying users; moreover, any form of corruption is absent, as recognized by the World Bank.[183]
- Even in Chile a good solution of PbWM is represented by EMOS, the Chilean company of Santiago which was privatized in *Aguas Andinas* just for budgetary reasons. Indeed, the public company was efficient and well run, both on the water supply aspect and on the sanitation one, as acknowledged by the WB.[184]

g Advantages and Criticisms of the Public Model

The advantages of a (well-operated) system of PbWM include the achievement of a more democratic decision-making process through contracts open to the public, strategies implemented by those bodies selected through democratic

179 Dourojeanni, supra note 147 at 13.
180 Sjölander Holland, supra note 6, at 187–188.
181 For further information see https://www.epm.com.co/.
182 For further information see http://www.etapa.net.ec/.
183 Sjölander Holland, supra note 6, at 183.
184 Ibid., at 182, 217.

elections, and transparency. Further, conflicts between social interests and private interests are likely to be avoided, and difficulties coordinating the private operator with state authorities are eliminated. Probably, the profits resulting from the service's provision will be reinvested in the system to improve it. The result will be that the municipalities' autonomy will be ensured.

The main problems identified in PbWM, among which the 'deviation' from the ideal form of water management, are exactly those reasons that induce governments to privatize and which determine the higher efficiency of the private water management. Often PbWM, even if it recognizes the RtW at an abstract level, lacks the necessary resources to effectively implement this right. Linked to the lack of adequate resources is the circumstance under which a state assumes too many responsibilities, instead of sharing them with the private operator, and often does not manage to fulfill all of them. Another element causing the resource deficit is the fact that the public operator is used to fix a low water tariff in order to avoid complaints, or to rarely augment them, even if there is the necessity of a higher tariff, because it knows that this will lead to demonstrations and diminution of political consensus. Lacking sufficient financial resources, there are not enough incentives to improve the efficiency of the water system. Furthermore, the situation is worsened by the registered excess of employees and the tendency to run into debt.[185] Finally, the water user is aware that, even if he/she does not comply with the obligation to pay the water bill, it is unlikely that the public provider will suspend the provision of water. These circumstances do not provide an incentive for users' compliance and worsen the problem of insufficient finances.

The deficiency of resources is often dealt with through 'special concessions' granted by the state to private operators under public governance, a circumstance that often creates inequality affecting competition. Moreover, political influence often threatens equal access to water, and the related risk of corruption is generally high.

A different equally important concern is that of the informal access to water, which is often ignored by the state or, although the state is aware of it, effective measures to address it are rarely implemented. The failure of the state in water management may also result from the fact that the state is often unable to protect the interests of weaker groups of water users, for example, farmers or indigenous groups, which have been deprived of water due to the water use demands of more powerful users.[186]

185 Massarutto, supra note 90, at 105–115, see Table at 108–109.

186 See Dourojeanni, supra note 158, at 52–60.

Finally, the circumstance whereby in the PbWM system the state is at the same time the controller (as a water responsible authority) and the controlled subject (as the water provider) is prone to cause a lack of effective control on the water provider's conduct, hence reducing the incentives to good behavior.

h Examples of Efficient Private Water Management

As regards the potential of PvWM, a few examples can be mentioned. The number of 'pure' private systems is very much lower than the number of public ones or PPPs.

- First, there is the exampale of La Paz, the capital of Bolivia, and El Alto, a poor neighborhood in the Bolivian capital. The water network management was granted to a private operator, *Aguas del Illimani*, in 1997 through a 30-year concession. This choice was made due to the degraded condition of the network and the politicization and inefficiency of the management. In addition, the water system lacked equity in terms of provison of water and sewage services. Therefore, one of the main conditions for the concession was the commitment to achieve equal access to water and to improve efficiency. The private company strictly complied with the requirements. It invested US$63 million to renew the infrastructure and built about 1,430 km of pipelines. The growth in coverage as regards both water provision and sanitation has been remarkable.[187] Investments have been focused in those areas with a more disadvantaged population in order to achieve equality. Moreover, the quality of the service has improved. The tariff, calculated in US dollars, was stable but, due to a 35% reduction of the Bolivian currency in relation to the dollar, 'increased' by the same amount, reducing people's capacity to pay their water bill.[188] However, subsequent developments and a negative conjuncture of factors (among others, the increase of the tariff) led to strong popular pressure, which caused the government to withdraw the concession in 2005.[189]
- A second example is that of Chilean economic development due to water privatization since the beginning of the 1980s. Specifically, Chile introduced the right to *own* water (which is very different from the right to have *access* to water), with the possibility to freely dispose of this right. The opening of the water market produced an increase in water availability in two respects.

---

187 A contrary opinion can be found in F. Laserre, *Acqua. Spartizione di una risorsa* (Milan: Ponte alle Grazie srl., 2004) at 174–175.

188 Segerfeldt, supra note 90, at 133–145, in particular see Table at 135.

189 For further information see ibid., at 133–145.

First, the water owners have been encouraged to reduce water consumption and to avoid wasting water because this will directly affect their profits. Secondly, the water prices were lowered due to the incremental increase in efficiency and the augmentation of available water. Two central factors that positively contributed to the success of the market were the establishment of the water price at a level similar to its real cost and a favorable conjunction of factors benefiting the Chilean economy in general.[190] Moreover, the flourishing of the sector has led to consistent investment in infrastructure; consequently, nearly all users are covered by the water service. In addition, private financial intervention allowed the country to become the biggest fruit exporter of the southern hemisphere. Indeed, from 1975 to 1990, agriculture productivity grew at the rate of 6% per year.[191]

i Advantages and Criticisms of the Private Model

In general, it can be affirmed that a series of advantages characterizes the PvWM. One of them, maybe the most acknowledged, is that the resources that the private operator owns is often considerably more than that belonging to the public body. This circumstance usually leads to investments aimed at improving the efficiency and management of the water network. These investments in the water sector may lead to a better compliance with environmental standards and thus result in a benefit for the country. Due to this availability of resources, the private operator can benefit the sector by providing modern and efficient technical and managerial knowledge, a competition-oriented approach, as well as lower prices over the long term due to improved efficiency.[192]

This higher amount of resources is often dependent, among other factors, on the fact that the tariff fixed by the private company is more 'realistic' as long as it better represents the real financial needs to ensure the stability of the company itself and, consequently, of the provision of water services.[193] What will be confuted is the assumption that a privatized system conflicts with social equity as a rule because, for example, it can be balanced with an efficient system of public subsidies to the poorest people.[194] Moreover, the control of the public authority over the provider is easier when water management

190 Ibid., at 53–56.

191 R. Bate, 'Let the Market Decide on Water Supply', *Mail & Guardian* (South Africa), (1 March 2001).

192 Segerfeldt, supra note 90, at 81–82, 147.

193 See Sjölander Holland, supra note 6, at 259.

194 Segerfeldt, supra note 90, at 76–78.

is privatized because the state, if it finds irregularities in the system, is not "denouncing" itself.[195]

The main concerns linked to water privatization are related to the power that a private operator could gain once they have obtained the concession for the service. One risk can be substitution of a public monopoly for a private one, exposing the market to eventual abuse, such as unfair increases in the water tariff.[196] The profits deriving from water management are often perceived by the general public as contrasting with the nature of water. Moreover, often the profits are not re-invested in the countries where the gain was produced to improve the domestic water infrastructure, to lower the water tariff or, at least, to benefit the domestic economy; rather, they 'flow' to other countries. Related to this latter concern is the fact that investments in a different currency, mainly in developing countries, are seen as a menace to the financial balance of the state and as a burden on the national economy.

Regarding the public element, PvWM often causes the state to 'abdicate' its duty to grant the RtW. Furthermore, the presence of the private element in the debate often reduces the space left for civic participation in decisions concerning water management. Yet, the lack of transparency on the concession contracts, and the creation of monopoly situations, affect the right of citizens to be informed on water politics. Concerns come also from the shift itself to PvWM. Indeed, not only for the high transaction costs of these transformations,[197] but also for the possible negative impacts on the right to collective bargaining for water workers.[198]

In addition, at this point it seems opportune to underline the issues generated by the particular model of granting water rights (WRs) to private stakeholders and, in general, by the recognition of water as a private good, as occurred in Chile. Dourojeanni identified the following series of concerns.[199] First, in this particular framework, the state is used to grant more WRs than the actual water availabile. Under this circumstance, the creation of 'paper rights' devaluates those water rights already granted. The latter water rights, despite having *juridical security*, lack of *water security*, as they do not correspond to available quantity of water. Second, once the state has given more WRs than the water availabile, it is, *in theory*, able to confiscate them (all the more if it has granted

195 Ibid., at 102.

196 Ibid., at 107.

197 Massarutto, supra note 90, at 105–115, see Table at 108–109.

198 Sjölander Holland, supra note 6, at 257–265.

199 Dourojeanni, supra note 158, at 52–60.

them for free, like in Chile) but, *in practice*, it cannot do so without having to face strong political consequences. Third, there is widespread concern related to the fact that water transactions generate many inequalities, which can be defined as 'water externalities', hence impeding the achievement of a fair and balanced allocation of water resources. Finally, this system is affected by a lack of prioritization of its inspiring values. Indeed, there is no priority given to water for human use (while it should be the first priority) in quantity and quality. On the contrary, potable water companies compete with all the other actors in the market. Furthermore, there is no environmental priority (while it should also be among the first priorities).

Despite these concerns, the legal acknowledgment of the water rights' market can be seen as a way to control this market because, even in the absence of formal recognition, it may grow in an informal and more dangerous way. The informal water market strongly affects weaker stakeholders, obliging them to buy water from private sellers at a much higher price than the price paid by users who have domestic access to water.[200]

j A Halfway Solution: The PPP and Some Examples

The half-way solution is the public-private partnership (PPP), considered by the majority of the actors involved in the issue as the most efficient solution, as it has the advantages of both options. Through this model, the public authority takes advantage of the resources owned by the private operator to improve the existing (publicly owned) infrastructure and its maintenance. A PPP can also utilize the private system of governance, which is often more advantageous from a budgetary point of view.[201]

The use of PPPs is constantly growing. Research to the end of 2007 has shown that the population served by private companies in developing and emerging countries grew from 94 million in 2000 to more than 160 million by the end of 2007. Since the beginning of the system's implementation in the 1990s, around 260 concession contracts have been awarded to private operators, of which 84% were still active at the end of 2007, while just 9% had been terminated early.[202] The Brazilian city of Recife, after rejecting the move

200 Segerfeldt, supra note 90, at 72–73, 76, in particular see Table at 73.

201 For an evaluation of the efficiency of PPPs see K. Ringskog, M. E. Hammond, & A. Locussol, *Using Management and Lease-Affermage Contracts for Water Supply. How Effective are They in Improving Service Delivery?*, World Bank Grid Lines No.12 (Washington, D.C.: Public-Private Advisory Facility, The World Bank, 2006).

202 P. Marin, *Public-Private Partnerships for Urban Water Utilities: A Review of Experiences in Developing Countries* (Washington, D.C.: The World Bank, 2009) at 2.

towards privatization due to a strong civic opposition, created an efficient PPP with important benefits for the renovation of infrastructure and governance.

A PPP is initiated by the public entity, which will advertise the need for the delivery of a particular service (in this case, the provision of water). A competitive process culminates in one competitor obtaining the right to deliver the service through a concession agreement. The private sector entity is called the 'project company' and is usually a new company, related to the winning company, but specifically aimed at fulfilling the delivery of the service and bearing its financial risk. This latter company is called a 'special purpose vehicle'.[203] An example of a particular form of PPP, which can be defined as 'a PPP beyond the traditional PPP', is the Chilean-Swiss project *SuizAgua*.[204]

k Advantages and Criticisms of the PPP

The framework of the PPP presents several advantages, which are mainly linked to the enhanced stability that this 'solution of compromise' represents. First, the PPPs are often planned to last over time and strategies are implemented with a long-term view. Generally, another relevant factor of their success is that the financial risk is transferred to the party that is more likely to properly manage it at the least cost. Further, the competitive selection process itself usually ensures the choice of the best offer and, therefore, of the most efficient partner.

The reciprocal transference of competencies and knowledge between the private operator and the public entity improves the efficiency of the service and encourages innovation. Notably, the service quality is often enhanced, in particular with regard to the reduction of water losses. Hence, operational efficiency and improved service quality are two crucial merits characterizing private involvement.[205] Yet, it is noteworthy that the PPP, despite being based on a public initiative, is not subject to political interference. Finally, as payment is often related to performance, the private operator has more incentive to constantly improve the quality of its service.

---

203 V. Tan, *The Public-Private Partnership (PPP)* (London: Advocates for International Development, 2012); E. Kleemeier & H. Lockwood, *Public-Private Partnerships for Rural Water Service*, Briefing Note No. 4 (The Hague: IRC International Water and Sanitation Centre, 2012) at 3; for a schematization see diagram at 6.

204 See the website for SuizAgua, http://www.suizagua.org/; see also A. C. Dourojeanni & C. Galleguillos, *SuizAgua Andina Chile: RSEAgua, un compromiso necesario para la Sustenabilidad* (Santiago de Chile: Fundación Chile, 2014).

205 Marin, supra note 202, at 7.

Recent studies (e.g. World Bank Group, 2016) confirm the positive trends registered in 2007 (supra, in previous sub-section). The PPP is, in general, still recognized as a successful choice for developing countries. Accordingly, the PPP model would help developing countries to better face the challenges of sustainability and financial viability of their water systems, overcoming the barriers of poor water supply and sanitation services and of constrained budgets. Moreover, the PPP would bring the promise to increase energy efficiency and water availability through non-revenue water management or through development of new water sources.[206]

In spite of these positive features,[207] there are disadvantages to a PPP. Primarily, its long-term nature can lead to debt for the private party long before the registration of the investment's benefits. If the private party becomes insolvent or abuses of its position under the concession agreement, this will cause negative political outcomes. The private operator may not invest the amount stated in the concession agreement and public funding is then required to complement the private action, which is what happened in Colombia.[208] Finally, the PPP contract is often the product of complex negotiations, which implies high transaction and legal costs. The resulting project will probably reflect the same complicated structure.[209]

As a final remark, it is difficult to judge the overall efficiency of the private partner's performance in the fulfillment of the concession agreement's obligations given that under those contracts the private partner is often responsible for both the implementation of operations and the investments. Therefore, research on the investments' adequateness should complement the analysis. It is for this reason that the use of 'hybrid' PPPs is growing: the outcome is a model of partnership which sees the private involvement focused on improving operational efficiency and service quality, whereas the public party is responsible for providing the most relevant part of the investment.[210]

In addition, an important element to consider is whether the water tariff level is settled according to public standards or private ones. Public utilities are often not adequately financed because the tariff adopted is lower than the

206 For more information see http://ppp.worldbank.org/public-private-partnership/5-trends-public-private-partnerships-water-supply-and-sanitation.

207 For a series of tables on the efficiency of PPPs see J. Jamieson, *PPP in Water and Sanitation: Don't Believe the Hype* (International Finance Corporation, 2010). In particular on the performance of PPPs in rural areas see Kleemeier & Lockwood, supra note 202.

208 See Marin, supra note 202, at 3.

209 Tan, supra note 203, at 5–6.

210 Marin, supra note 202, at 8.

cost-recovery level and this deficit affects efficiency, making users even less willing to pay their bill (despite it being low) for inefficient service. Instead, a water tariff that reflects the cost-recovery level will have positive outcomes on efficiency, thus creating incentives for the users' willingness to pay.[211]

1 Shared Issues in Both Models: Different Water Law, but Similar Issues

From the parallel analysis of the public and private models for water management, the resulting scenario is characterized by very different legal water frameworks. However, these different frameworks are rarely affected by problems so dissimilar. This means that in some way the recognition of water as a common-pool resource and the prohibition of privatized management does not avoid those issues that are linked to the governance of water, whatever the legal statements on water affirm. This circumstance suggests that there are factors which cannot be changed only by legal modifications, and that any legal analysis should take into account those factors.

Considering a set of solutions which goes from one extreme scenario (recognition of water as a common-pool resource and prohibition of its privatization in the constitution, e.g. Uruguay) to another (water's suitability to become private property affirmed in the constitution, e.g., Chile), the following shared issues can be underlined. First, the externalities caused by water transactions are rarely handled by the state in a proper way: in countries that recognize water as a common good, there is no provision for water market's consequences on third parties because this water market is not supposed to exist, but *de facto* these externalities occur, beyond the normative framework. In countries without this recognition, such as Chile, where, within the Water Code, there is a norm providing that water transactions cannot harm third parties, the existence of a water market is recognized, but this provision is just 'dead letter', i.e. there is no compliance with this norm by the majority of the stakeholders involved.

Another concern is the controversial matter of water allocation, which is often resolved by granting more water to the most politically or economically powerful stakeholders. This circumstance occurs both in systems with public water management (it occurs *de facto*), as in Ica, Peru, and in systems with privatized water management, as in Copiapó, Chile (here it happens legally).

Furthermore, both models are deficient in the proper self-regulation by the main operator (the state or the private company) in order to allocate water equally, to preserve the environment of the river basin, to avoid surface and

211 Ibid., at 5.

subterranean water exploitation, and to grant the quantity and quality of water required to meet people's needs. Another weakness affecting the two systems is the general lack of adequate information about the context in which the actions related to water management are implemented. The third deficit is represented by the low or, even, non-existing civic involvement in the water management decision-making process, a circumstance that causes civic dissatisfaction and complaints once resolutions are made.

The two models present many differences. The most relevant divergence regards accountability. In the public model, the state should be responsible for executing actions and regulating itself to achieve water equality. In contrast, under the private model, the state has to be a regulator, impinging on the sector just to subsidize those users lacking sufficient access to water or sufficiently good water quality. Instead, the main responsibility with respect to all those requirements, first, rests on the private operator and then, just at a subsidiary level, belongs to the state.[212]

However, some insight can be gleaned from both the systems to improve each of them, despite their differences. They both need to be revised to achieve more efficient management, which would benefit from higher technical knowledge and a deeper awareness on the context of action. Moreover, as it is clear from the preceding analysis, effective participation must be considered. At least, these systems should implement some form of citizens' consultation in the decision-making process related to water governance. At the same time, they both require the state to control itself (in the case of public management) or the private operator (in the case of private management), and the users to control the state (in the case of public management) or the state and the private operator (in the case of private management).

It is clear from the above discussion that *none of the models* can be considered to be the best solution to gain water equality. Arguably, an exemplary model of 'good' water management does not exist, because water is also a cultural good and each society has its own culture of water, historically developed on a territorial, social, economic, and political basis. Therefore, the desperate search for one model for water management to be implemented everywhere is useless and unwise. On the contrary, only the responsible and aware management of existing local structures can contribute to the achievement of a good water system.[213]

However, despite the impossibility of establishing a general model water system considered as the best option for every context, a balanced solution

---

212 Dourojeanni, supra note 158, at 52–60.

213 Hachfeld et al., supra note 164, at 4.

that is more likely to have a positive outcome may be the PPP. This is due to its particular structure, which embraces the advantages of both systems and thus mitigates the criticisms of each one-sided solution. However, the PPP model *per se* is neither perfect nor complete. Indeed, it should be complemented with forms of involvement of civil society and with a high level of technical and managerial knowledge.

m The Factors Affecting the Outcome of a System, whether Public or Private

It is extremely difficult and unrealistic to evaluate the efficiency and pertinence of a system just by looking at its legal features. This last element is important, but it must be complemented by an analysis of the context in which it is inserted. The relevant factors affecting outcomes for a water management system (whether public or private) essentially are dependent on the water law, the institutional framework, the culture and history of the country, the geographic and, specifically, hydrographic features of an area. As regards the last point, it is important to specify the presence or absence of a situation of water scarcity, or even drought, as this has a strong role in shaping the issues of the sector, because the concern of granting water to every user will somehow monopolize the debate and the politics of water management.

The following reasons seem to be crucial for the success of a water system, whether public or private. First, a central factor is the stability of the state: the private actor is more willing to invest in a state that presents a guarantee of economic and political stability of the water sector and, in general, of the public economy and finance; consequently, both public and private water companies are strongly affected by political and economic instability of a state.

Another determinant element is the capacity of the operator: the amount of technical knowledge and means available to the company and a wise use of them are crucial for its success. This second circumstance is linked to that of good governance[214] of the technical and economic resources belonging to the company, as well as of the conflicts over water management that always arise in each kind of system.

Finally, the good condition of the infrastructure allows a balanced choice between the public and the private operator (the public actor is not forced to privatize because it does not have sufficient resources to improve the water network). If private management is chosen, it will not increase the tariff in

---

214 The importance of focusing on water governance instead of the water market was underlined by Carl Bauer, VII Jornadas de Derecho ambiental, 15 October 2014, Santiago de Chile.

order to recover the costs linked to the renewal of the network (a circumstance which often causes civic opposition to privatization), but it will probably fix prices at a level comparable to that of public management. For this reason, nowadays private firms prefer to invest in countries that already have complete and functioning infrastructures.[215]

At this stage, the question of what a good water system entails can be answered thanks to the lessons learnt from Latin America. Such system shall achieve and be based on

- water security;
- good quality of water;
- operational efficiency,[216] which is represented by a good control of water losses, efficient bill collection, and high labor productivity;
- equity in water access, which means a water tariff based on the financial capacity of each individual;
- universality and continuity of the service, which implies that disconnection of private households must be considered illegal;
- a fair allocation of economic and technical resources;
- effective civic engagement and effectiveness in meeting public needs, which must be defined, monitored, and evaluated through participatory democratic processes;
- solidarity in the guarantee of the RtW, which implies that water companies should not only look at the concerns of their geographic area, but also beyond their context to share knowledge and even to support companies with less financial resources and technical competence;
- sustainability in the long term of the solutions achieved, supported by progressive legislation, which follows and adapts itself to the context's mutations;
- protection of biodiversity, and preservation of water resources and of the water cycles; and
- use of IRBM as the tool to achieve these goals.[217]

As regards the last point, a timely statement by Hackfeld et al. could be regarded as the closing lesson: 'We do not own water; we only borrow it from nature. It is our responsibility to make sure that we use water only in responsible quantities, do not pollute it and give it back to the water cycle at a high quality'.[218]

215 Jampaglia & Molinari, supra note 90, at 109.

216 Marin, supra note 202, 20.

217 Hachfeld et al., supra note 164, at 5–6; Dourojeanni, supra note 158, at 52–60.

218 Ibid., at 5.

n The Need for Pragmatism in the Debate

An urgent demand for pragmatism in the handling of water matters has arisen in recent decades mainly due to the proliferation of national and international official statements proclaiming rights linked to water and the environment. Ideology should be left aside in this field, because it is urgent to focus the debate on specific issues rather than on general statements. The discussion, however, seems only limitedly improved by these national and supranational contributions. Arguably, the most important factors that should be considered in planning water strategies (like the social, technical and environmental aspects) are often disregarded, and attention tends to be focused on abstract statements.

Often misunderstandings and misleading affirmations dominate the discussion. For example, it is different to argue that the water service *management* can be entrusted to a private operator by a specific concession and for a set time, than rhetorically affirming that water can be "sold" to a private company. Yet, water cannot be given *for free*: any movement asking for this guarantee is just unrealistic and unaware that the costs of water provision cannot be borne by the state alone.[219] It should be remembered that the right to water is not an unlimited right (see Part A above): one of these limits is that the state or the enterprise has to recover the costs of supplying water. Moreover, the technical knowledge and the amount of financial resources required to properly manage the water network are not always available to the public sector. Therefore, forms of interaction with the private sector are advisable.

In conclusion, it is not useful to design the best water law only by making abstract statements. Rather, it is necessary to design a good strategy in order to achieve an efficient water management for each river basin with clear objectives with regards to climate change, coastal management, IWRM, and other key areas. The likely counterargument is that the water issue should be dealt with by a general approach because it affects the whole society. Following this belief, it is indispensable for the relevant authorities to state general and strict principles to grant the right to water to every human being, regardless the context in which he/she lives, and this only can be done by the state at the highest level. Arguably, this approach provides homogeneity in the solutions implemented, but it does not consider that water issues can change substantially from place to place, and from one community to another. Conclusively, it can be argued that tailor-made strategies are preferable to one-size-fits-all approaches to water governance.

219 Sjölander Holland, supra note 6, at 131,133, 206.

C Insight into the Chilean Water Framework

It has been stressed in the previous chapters that the debate on the RtW cannot disregard the analysis of the role of the private sector, which can be considered—on one hand—as a contributor to the achievement of the RtW, but—on the other hand—as a threat to it. The private sector it is often alleged to be responsible for violations of the RtW. This suggests the need to focus on the controversial relationship between the RtW and the private water sector through an outstanding example, namely that of Chile, which probably has the most privatized water framework.

I *Article 19 of the Chilean Constitution and the Political Context of 1980*

In order to address the Chilean legal scenario for water, it is crucial to mention the Constitution of 1980, which is still in force. Indeed, this fundamental text directly shapes the formulation of the 1981 Water Code, but also affects the opportunities for any government to modify the strict market-based approach for water allocation.[220] Indeed, despite the process of re-democratization that has followed the "Pinochet era", the neoliberal economic model developed under his dictatorship endures in Chilean society and is still profoundly reflected in its constitution. That means that the multiparty coalition, the *Concertación* of the following years (1990 to 2013), composed of Christian Democratic and Moderate Socialist presidents (among the latter belongs the current president Michelle Bachelet, who is close to the end of her mandate), has not really overturned the economic scenario, which is based on a highly privatized approach. Indeed, as one author affirmed, the *Concertación* 'has done little to overcome the arrangement of inequality inherited from the dictatorship'.[221] The state-sponsored neo-liberalism causes Chilean society to be 'one of the most unequal in the world' with consistent segments of the population excluded from the benefits of the market.[222] In 2013, the *Concertación* was replaced by the New Majority coalition (*Nueva Mayoría*).

An emblem of this market approach is Article 19(21) of the Constitution, which guarantees to all persons 'the right to develop any economic activity' as long as 'it is not contrary to morals, public order or national security, abiding [by] the legal norms which regulate it'. The possibility for the state to be entrepreneur is permitted, but a certain procedure is required:

---

220 Sáez -Muñoz, supra note 4, at 128.

221 B. Loveman, *Chile: The Legacy of Hispanic Capitalism* (Oxford: Oxford Universiy Press, 2001) at 343–346.

222 Alexander, supra note 32, at 12.

> The State and its bodies may develop entrepreneurial activities or participate therein only provided that such activities or such participation are authorized by a law passed by a qualified quorum. In such case, those activities shall be subjected to the common legislation applicable to private individuals, without prejudice to exceptions for justifiable motives established by a law, being also passed by a qualified quorum.[223]

Yet, in subsection 24 of the same Article, property rights are assured in their diverse aspects over all classes of corporeal and incorporeal goods. Nevertheless, the law—but only the law—may limit the right given the social function of that property. Further, subsection 24 provides a constitutional guarantee for the owner of a mining concession and for the rights of private citizens over water, which grants a true *proprietorship* to the owners of water rights, as will be explained below.[224]

The relation between private property's limits and the protection of the environment, even if without specific mention to water resources, is stated in Article 19(8). The Article provides for the right to live in an environment free from contamination as well as the duty of the state to ensure the protection of this right. Most importantly, the following provision affirms that the law may establish specific restrictions on the exercise of certain rights or freedoms in order to protect the environment.[225]

223 Chile, Constitución Política de 1980, art.19(22).

224 Ibid., art. 19(24): '*La Constitución asegura a todas las personas*: 24°-(1) *El derecho de propiedad en sus diversas especies sobre toda clase de bienes corporales o incorporales. Sólo la ley puede establecer el modo de adquirir la propiedad, de usar, gozar y disponer de ella y las limitaciones y obligaciones que deriven de su función social.... Nadie puede, en caso alguno, ser privado de su propiedad, del bien sobre que recae o de alguno de los tributos o facultades esenciales del dominio, sino en virtud de ley general o especial que autorice la expropiación por causa de utilidad pública o de interés nacional, calificada por el legislador....*(9) *El dominio del titular sobre su concesión minera está protegido por la garantía constitucional de que trata este número....* (11) *Los derechos de los particulares sobre las aguas, reconocidos o constituidos en conformidad a la ley, otorgarán a sus titulares la propiedad sobre ellos ...*'.

225 Ibid., art.19(8): '*La Constitución asegura a todas las personas: 8°- El derecho a vivir en un medio ambiente libre de contaminación. Es deber del Estado velar para que este derecho no sea afectado y tutelar la preservación de la naturaleza. La ley podrá establecer restricciones específicas al ejercicio de determinados derechos o libertades para proteger el medio ambiente ...*'.

II *Elements of Reflection*

In Chile, the protection of private property is firmly stated mainly because this right is part of an historic *acquis* recognized by every democratic constitution. Its constitution affirms its value and its inviolability, but not unconditionally; this means that the state retains at any time the faculty to limit the enjoyment of the right in the name of the general interest.

Nevertheless, in Chile it is unlikely that the state will intervene on private interests to defend the public interest due to its scarce willingness to impinge on private properties. This verification is more evidence that the legal data often does not properly reflect the factual reality. Moreover, it is quite remarkable that Chilean Law explicitly affirms the possibility of private property restriction in the name of environmental protection. However, again, in practice, this power can be considerably restricted.

III *The Particularities of the Chilean Model*

Any analysis of the Chilean water situation shall start from a reflection on the country's unique shape: the country stretches 2,600 miles but it is just 220 miles wide. While on the northern part stands the driest desert in the world, the Atacama Desert, the south has extremely abundant of water because it receives from 80 to 270 inches of precipitation per year.

On the whole, Chile is a country with a high amount of water per capita: 56,000 m^3 of water per person per year that is about seven times the world average. Notwithstanding this fact, the resource is not homogeneously allocated: in the north the average is less than 2,000 m^3 of water per person per year.[226] This discrepancy is also reflected in the price of the preferred water stocks: in the north, the water stocks may cost up to 6,028,000 Chilean pesos (equivalent to 10,000) dollars due to the water scarcity, whereas in the south their general cost is no more than 60,280 Chilean pesos (equivalent to 100 dollars).[227] The central area presents a middle way situation, with its Mediterranean and temperate climate. Therefore, the central issue is to bring water as well as energy linked to water exploitation (through hydroelectric plants), from the south to the north, where not only the population but even the enterprises—mainly the mines—need it.

It is exactly the mining sector the leading exports and revenues generator in Chile, having consequently a strong power in orienting water-related decisions. At the same time, the mining sector is responsible for large water use,

---

226 Interview with Wilfredo Alfaro Catalán, Ingeniero Forestal, Corporación Nacional Forestal—CONAF, Ministerio de Agricoltura, 7 October 2014, Santiago de Chile.

227 Ibid.

which has been conducted without sufficient regard for sustainability. In the north of Chile, the businesses using water have often deprived rural communities of the dispensable amount of the already scarce water. Differently, in the south, the mining sector has had an impact on glaciers, building roads and tunnels through them.

Also, the usage of water within the country is quite inhomogeneous: on the total water withdrawal, which accounts to about 2,000 m^3/s of water, the majority (85%) of the consumptive water use is for irrigation due to the importance of the Chilean agricultural sector, while just the restant amount is shared among industrial, mining, and human uses. The non-consumptive use is dominated by hydroelectric generation, which represents 68% percent of water use. The Chilean energy sector is dominated by water, the hydroelectric potential of the country being extremely high (18,000 MW). The rapidity of allocation of these non-consumptive WRs and the speculation over them is worrisome.[228]

In order to understand the current role of private enterprises using water in Chile, it is opportune to reflect firstly on the uniqueness of the scenario, which has been called 'the Chilean Model'[229] for its particular approach studied worldwide. Under the Pinochet dictatorship, a single water regime was created: it holds the record to be the most *laissez-faire* in the world. The Inter-American Development Bank and the World Bank have encouraged numerous countries to follow this model.

According to the Chilean water regime, the state owns the resource but it can entrust individuals with 'water rights', which precisely are rights of advantageous use (*derechos de aprovechamiento*). Now, it is important to remember the difference between the WRs whose competence belongs to the *Dirección General de Aguas* (the General Water Management), and the duty of the state to ensure the right to water,[230] although not mandated in the Constitution. This latter duty belongs to the *Superintendencia de Servicios Sanitarios* (Superintendence of Sanitary Services).[231]

The water itself remains under state ownership, but the public authorities are no longer able to freely decide on the use of the resource. This unfettered use receives a constitutional recognition under Article 19(3) of the Chilean Constitution where it is expressly affirmed that 'the rights of private citizens

228 R. R. Hearne & G. Donoso, '*Water Institutional Reforms in Chile*', Water Policy Vol. 7 (2005), pp. 53–69 at 54, 62, 63.

229 Brown, supra note 97; Sáez-Muñoz, supra note 4, at 13, 14, 20, 95.

230 T. R. Lee & A. Jouravlev, *Prices, Property and Market in Water Allocation* (Santiago de Chile: CEPAL, 1998).

231 For more information on the *Superintendencia de Servicios Sanitarios* see http://www.siss.cl.

over water, recognized and constituted in conformity with the law, shall grant proprietorship to the owners thereof'. The constitutional reinforcement of the WR protection is unique and distinguishes Chile from the other LA countries.[232]

What will be discussed in this paragraph is the right on water when granted to private businesses. In Chile, the state has been indulgent in conceding WRs to entrepreneurs who needed it for their corporate aims. Not only have the rights been profusely allocated, they have also been given for free. This represented a smart maneuver for incentivizing foreign firms to invest in the country, and has accelerated the economic growth of the country, but at the same time it has disregarded the adverse impact on the environment.

The discussed scenario has been called 'the schizophrenia'[233] of the Chilean Constitution. Indeed, those who are granted with WRs have an unregulated faculty to dispose of a proclaimed common good such as water. However, part of the legal doctrine does not recognize this contradiction: according to this perspective, the resource is considered a common good, but *only when it flows from the spring*; immediately after that moment, it is susceptible to become private property.[234]

At this stage it is important to draw a distinction between water as a resource and water as a natural element. The first is suitable to serve private needs and therefore to fall within the denomination of private property, with the possibility to generate 'rights to use water'. The second is to be classified as a common-pool resource belonging, first of all, to the environment and, secondly, to the overall society.

IV *The Chilean Case from an Historical Perspective*

The singular approach of the Water Code of 1981,[235] as well as of the 1980 Constitution, both currently in force, is to be found in the influence of the dictatorship but, more specifically, to the contribution of the 'Chicago Boys',[236] a group of Chilean economists which studied at the University of Chicago's School of Economics (between the 1950s and the 1960s) in order to design an innovative solution for the Chilean economy. The principal outcome was a unique market-oriented system in which the state role in water allocation was reduced on behalf of the market. This extreme free-market approach was

232 Dourojeanni & Jouravlev, supra note 93, at 10.

233 Catalán Interview, supra note 226.

234 J. H. Zañartu Rosselot, '*Aguas subterráneas: ¿Necesidad de un nuevo enfoque?*', Revista de Derecho Administrativo Económico de Recursos Naturales, Vol.3(2) (2001), pp. 539–545.

235 Chile, Código de Aguas (Water Code), 13 August 1981, D.F.L. Nº 1.122.

236 More information can be found in Sáez-Muñoz, supra note 4, at 138–144.

justified as an indispensable recovery for the Chilean economy after Allende's government.

The experiment made Chile the earliest and most acclaimed case of neoliberal orthodoxy realized in a developing country in Latin America.[237] It can be affirmed that the influence of the Chicago Boys is still present in the Chilean water scenario in so far as the economic interests keep determining governmental choices.[238]

The idea is to replace the role of the state in order to assign a central position to private investors, which consequently receive strong powers on water-related decisions. The resulting water market is, generally, a competitive and free market. The state still detains a role, even if subsidiary, to enact a regulatory and legislative framework in order to coordinate and promote private initiatives. Because of the historical reputation of Latin American water administrations, notorious for their inefficiencies, the Chilean approach was attractive for many businesses.

In particular, according to the Code, these rights were granted in perpetuity, free of charge, and susceptible to being inherited like any other type of property but, differently from the traditional property, they were not taxed: they could be freely traded, mortgaged and transferred.[239] Article 5 of the Water Code grants the right to use the WRs in accordance with the provisions of the Code. The faculty to exploit those rights is further stated in Article 6. The rights holders have a wide discretion on how to use 'their' water. It is noteworthy that there is no requirement to make use of the resource which, at the same time, benefits the society. Actually, there was no requirement to use the right at all, before the Reform of 2005, as it will be explained hereinafter.

The favor towards the ownership of WRs is evident. It is crystallized in the Code and in the Constitution,[240] also considering the fact that the limits of this property are few. One of the limits consists of not infringing upon third parties' rights. Two other limits to this unregulated scenario are represented by

237 Alexander, supra note 32, at 4.

238 R. Lüders, *La Misión Klein-Saks, los Chicago Boys y la Política Económica*, Documento de Trabajo IE-PUC, No. 411 (Santiago: Pontificia Universidad Catolica de Chile, Instituto de Economia, 2012); J. Díaz, R.Lüders, & G. Wagner, *Economía Chilena 1810–2000. Producto Total y Sectorial. Una Nueva Mirada*, Documento de Trabajo IE-PUC, No. 315 (Santiago: Pontificia Universidad Catolica de Chile, Instituto de Economia, 2007).

239 W. L. Alexander (ed.), *Lost in the Long Transition: Struggles for Social Justice in Neoliberal Chile*, (Lanham, MD: Lexington Books, 2009), at 43.

240 Chile, Constitución Política de 1980, art. 24: '*Los derechos de los particulares sobre las aguas, reconocidos o constituidos en conformidad a la ley, otorgarán a sus titulares la propiedad sobre ellos*'.

the provisions that WRs' owners cannot freely change the location of use and that new water rights—even if WRs are almost totally assigned—are subjected to some limited environmental flow requirements.

Yet, the users of WRs are not required to compensate for the eventual externalities they generate on third parties. The Code expressly considers water mainly as an economic good because the only instrument which it envisages for regulation is the water market. Disputes that eventually arise between WR holders are settled under the civil law, before civil courts. Moreover, in Article 10, the negation of the principle of inherency is underlined. WRs are separated from traditional land rights, a circumstance that is considered the cause of many conflicts between land owners and WR owners.

Another interesting point is represented by Article 14 of the Code, which creates the singular category of 'non-consumptive' water rights. Such rights allow the use of water, but it has to be returned to its source without being reduced in quantity and quality. Arguably, it is extremely difficult to give back water without altering it.

The Water Code explicitly draws the distinction between the two types of rights. Article 13 defines 'consumptive use rights' as those 'that entitles the holder of said right to totally consume the water in any activity.' Article 14 limits the 'non-consumptive use rights' to 'the use of water without consuming it'. Further, 'the extraction or restitution of the waters is to be done in a manner that does not harm the rights of third parties constituted over the same waters in terms of quantity, quality, substance, opportunity of use …'.

The innovation can be understood in the light of the need to create new WRs for future uses. Indeed, in the majority of the country's territory, the WRs are almost all already assigned and in use, without respecting the need of a minimum ecological flow (*caudal ecológico mínimo*) of water.[241]

This situation represents somehow the replacement of that of the '*merced de fuerza motriz*' (grant of driving force) of the previous Code, according to which the water use could be conceded for the production of electricity through hydroelectric plants. The introduction of the category arguably reflected the economic pressure of the powerful hydropower corporation Endesa, which demanded more and more water to satisfy the growing energy demands of the country.

A step towards the recognition of a certain minimum quantity of water volume was recognized in the Water Code Reform of 2005.[242] The reform

241 Speech of Luis Simón Figueroa, III Convención Nacional de Regantes de Chile, Los Angeles, 5–6 November 1993, Santiago de Chile, Confederación de Canalistas de Chile.

242 Chile, Reforma del Código de Aguas, 11 May 2005, Ley N° 20.017.

introduced the president of the Republic's cabinet the right to deny a request for new WRs if it threatens the essential amount of water available for human use and if exceptional circumstances of national interest arise. It is also possible to reserve formerly-owned WRs if the same requisites are present. Prior to October 2014, 24 decrees have been issued on the basis on this provision within nine of them justified by environmental concerns. This tool may be considered an efficient instrument to grant the protection of the environment in certain situations, but the narrow requisites make its use extremely rare.[243]

Differently from the United States where a WRs market exists, but is regulated with respect to environmental requirements, in Chile, nothing similar happens. Indeed, in the United States, the transfer of WRs and any modification in its use are conditional to the attaining of administrative approval in order to consider the eventual risks for the environment and the claims of the other rights' holders. A priority in the allocation of the resource is held by human users. For example, if in a certain area a company asks for a quantity of WRs but supplies are insufficient to satisfy the municipal and domestic use, this request is likely to be rejected.

In the Chilean system, there are no restrictions on the transfer of WRs, which can be bought and sold as freely as any type of real property. The public administration leaves the market to freely regulate itself, disregarding the environmental concerns, which call for limits to water speculation.[244] Yet, there are no usage priorities: all the stakeholders compete at the same level in the allocation of water. The result is that the most powerful interest groups are likely to be rural users. Moreover, just a minority, about 30%,[245] of Chilean WRs are formalized and recorded in the WRs' Register held by the state; the others are out of its control.

It is now interesting to briefly consider the antecedent of the 1981 Water Code: the first Water Code is that of 1951, which expressly recognized the suitability of WRs to form private property even if under fixed-term concessions and for specified uses. Subsequently, due to the influence of the 1967 Agrarian Reform Law, which reinstated government control over land, also considered water to be 'national property for public use' by amending the 1925 Constitution and the Water Code. The existing WRs were expropriated by the state without compensation. The Pinochet military coup brought back land

243 Speech of Francisco Puelma in the VII Jornadas de Derecho Ambiental, '*Recursos Naturales: ¿Sustentabilidad o Sobreexplotación?*', Aula Magna, Facultad de Derecho, Universidad de Chile, Pío Nono 1, Santiago de Chile, 15 October 2014.

244 Brown, supra note 97, at 3.

245 Catalán Interview, supra note 226.

to private owners, but only dealt with the water issue later, in the 1980s; therefore, for a certain period, the national water law and the neo-liberal approach co-existed.[246]

V The Chilean Model Today

Nowadays, the Chilean model is constantly under criticism. In particular, President Michelle Bachelet, in office since March 2014 (after her previous mandate from 2006 to 2010), has been committed to a series of reforms that involved the Water Code as well as numerous other sectors like education, labor, and taxes. In the specific field of water, the policy is based on the acknowledgment of the water stress situation that the country is going through. Climate change will bring more frequent droughts, and the country is not prepared to face them. Sustainable management of the water resource is considered the only option for the future endurance of the Chilean economy, but it is not easy to eradicate a model that is as entrenched as the Chilean model is. In view of the challenges represented by severe droughts and over-utilization of certain basins, the reform advanced by Bachelet proposed amendments to the current water legislative framework to secure state ownership of water resources and revoke current unused or misused water rights.

One of the first steps to achieve this change is represented by the appointment of a presidential delegate (*Delegado Presidencial*) with the specific responsibilty for water policies. In the Chilean system a presedential delegate is an institutional position, who can be appointed and removed freely by the President of the Republic, acting as the President's natural and immediate representative in the territory of his/her territorial jurisdiction or, in the case of the delegate appointed specifically for overseeing the water sector (*Delegado Presidencial para los Recursos Hídrico*), in the area of his/her thematic jurisdiction. An economic and agricultural expert was selected to this purpose, Reinaldo Ruiz. Mr. Ruiz's approach is inclined to consider water as a common-pool resource. In addition, a declaration about the public nature of water already exists within the Chilean legal system, as explained above. Notwithstanding, the rights of water use are unlimited in the sense that state's ownership of the resource is somehow meaningless and ineffective.

Behind the revocation of WRs is hidden a fear: a wave of nationalization that could frighten investors and discourage them from entering the Chilean market or, worse, make the companies present in the territory leave the country. The fear is related to the severe financial crisis faced by Chile in 1970 due to Allende's redistributive policies. The supporters of reform have said that the return to the state of water, which already belongs to the nation, does not

246 Alexander, supra note 239, at 42.

mean nationalization. Nonetheless, if the attention is focused on the privatized water system, it is impossible not to see certain equivalence in this manoeuvre.

Another remarkable initiative, which seems a step towards prioritization of human concerns over the market, is represented by the Indigenous Law of 1993.[247] In particular, Article 64 affirms that new WRs affecting the water resources that are ancestral property of indigenous communities can be created or assigned only with the guarantee that the provision of water to these communities will not be altered.

As already said, the Chilean Water Code of 1981 has been subjected to reform proposals several times, but no one reform has been decisive enough to reshape the Chilean model.[248] In particular, a 2005 reform[249] succeeded in amending the text, but only modestly. Additionally, the reform was extremely difficult to achieve after 13 years of parliamentary debates on it. The most remarkable innovation has been the provision for a payment (*patente por no uso*) due by the owners of WRs who do not effectively use them. The aim of the measure is to reduce speculation over WRs.[250] However, for a substantial change in the Chilean water framework, it is necessary also to amend the Constitution in order to remove the existing constitutional protections of private WRs.[251]

North pointed out that any water reform in Chile is essentially driven by ideological concerns.[252] The most evident example is that of the reform which has produced the current Chilean water system. In the 1981's reform, the neoliberal ideology supported by the military regime was evident. It was based on the defense of private property and on the restrictions of the state role in the market.

The main reforms needed to the actual Chilean water scenario are the reinforcement of the role of the water users' associations[253] to help them to properly face water shortages or floods, for example, by planning renovations of hydraulic infrastructure. Technically speaking, what it is most requested is the development of integrated water resource management as well as a water system that is takes into account climate change concerns. Organizations of

---

247 Chile, Ley Indigena No. 19.253, 5 October 1993.

248 See C. Bauer, 'Los Derechos de Agua y el Mercado: Efectos e implicancias del código de aguas chileno de 1981', IV&V *Revista de Derecho de Aguas* (1993) 17–63.

249 Chile, Reforma del Código de Aguas, Ley No. 20.017, 11 May 2005.

250 Catalán Interview, supra note 226.

251 Brown, supra note 97, at 4.

252 D. North, *Institutions, Institutional Change and Economic Performance* (Cambridge: Cambridge University Press, 2004).

253 See S. M. A. Salman, *The Legal Framework for Water Users' Associations: A Comparative Study*, World Bank Technical Paper no. 360 (Washington, D.C.: The World Bank, 1997).

water users have a sector-limited approach, i.e. they tend to be focused on the narrow area of their 'section' of a river or on their particular need for water, e.g. agriculture, hydropower, or urban use.[254]

The creation of river basin organizations to provide tailor-made strategies to deal with the issues facing each river is highly recommended. What is also important is the introduction of authorities for transboundary river basins because of the number of rivers shared with neighboring states. In addition, more pervasive control over groundwater is urgent. The contamination of rivers and lakes must also be kept under check through constant and efficient monitoring. It is necessary to plan strategies and implement tools to deal with the numerous conflicts among users, which have been worsened by the severe episodes of drought. Moreover, at an institutional level, the need to improve coordination between the different institutions involved in water governance must be stressed.

Lastly, the social importance of acknowledging the priority of water rights for human consumption cannot be neglected. Those communities located along the lower part of a river often are affected by not receiving enough water because it is overused by sectors upstream. Those claiming water for agricultural production are not prioritized over companies using water for industrial purposes. In particular, the hydropower plants often use water for generating electricity, disregarding the quantity of water that should be left for agriculture.

What is surprising is that many problems of the Chilean water scenario are analogous to countries which have the opposite type of water law, for example, problems such as contamination of river water, overexploitation of groundwater, and reductions in the size of glaciers. The situation of water stress that Chile is now facing has stimulated the proposal and the implementation of various solutions, such as the *SuizAgua* Project.[255] For its part, the government has invested in hydraulic infrastructure to improve their management and maintenance of water resources, as well as in alternative ways to obtain water. The building of desalination plants, the transport of water by undersea pipes along the Pacific coast, and water reuse initiatives in the mining sector are just some of the remarkable examples of this commitment.[256]

---

254 Dourojeanni Interview, supra note 129.

255 See http://www.suizagua.org/.

256 F. Donoso & R. Fuster, *Crisis del agua: diagnóstico y propuestas a partir de los consesos de la Iniciativa Agua y Medio Ambiente*, Andess Chile, Santiago de Chile, September 2014.

Conclusion: Lessons from Latin America

I *A Very Different Constitutional Scenario, but Common Unresolved Issues*

In Parts A and B it has been demonstrated that countries sometimes present diverse legal frameworks as regards the protection of water resources and the environment. Nevertheless, they share many similarities when it comes to water and environmental problems.

This leads to the conclusion that often the proclamation in, mainly recent, constitutions of the right to water and to a healthy environment has not been sufficient to secure the respect for some additional but indispensable principles. This does not mean that the inclusion of these rights in a constitution has been useless. Indeed, such formal statements are now strengthened by the particular legal force of that constitutional provision. Therefore, the acknowledgement in the constitution of these two rights represents an important step to better guarantee them. Nonetheless, the hypothesis advanced in this monograph is that often this recognition is not enough.

First of all, it is advisable that constitutionally recognized rights are implemented through more flexible legal tools like laws or regulations. Furthermore, it is important that this constitutional declaration is sustained by the definition and compliance with the already mentioned principles that are indispensable to avoid that the proclaimed rights remain abstract statements on paper.

These principles[257] should be regarded as a prerequisite for any project for efficiently managing the resource. First, water access for human use should be prioritized. Moreover, both the economic and the social value of water should be recognized as indispensable in the planning of water-related strategies that are financially sustainable but at the same time acceptable for society. The allocation of water to users such as peasants and indigenous communities should be protected. Lastly, it is important to create a water culture to make people aware of water risks and of appropriate practices, as well to encourage citizens' participation in water-related decision-making.

Furthermore, some guidelines should be respected in planning a water system: its future sustainability, on both an environmental and economic level, efficiency in water use, integrated water resource management, planning of strategies at the river basin level, and decentralization of water management, where public, from the central administration. Ultimately, the water stress should be dealt with using a precautionary approach rather than a reparative one.

257 Dourojeanni, supra note 147, at 61.

II *The Importance of Depoliticizing Water-Related Decisions*

The interference of political interests in water policy-making is often one of the main factors of inefficiencies and additional costs. Indeed, policy-makers are rarely as impartial as technicians and risk falling into the temptation to orient decisions to their political party's interests rather than for the common well-being. In addition, the risk of corruption of the politicians involved in granting water concessions is worrisome, as proved by the need for the adoption of the 2005 United Nations Convention against Corruption.[258]

A 1987 study conducted by the World Bank economist Gabriel Roth demonstrated that when politics predominates in certain sectors, as in natural monopolies, the likely outcome will be economic distortion, which he called 'governmental failures', creating an analogy with the parallel concept of 'market failures'.[259] This negative effect is mainly due to the fact that politics badly allocates resources and does not tend to maximize the benefit that is derived from the resource's exploitation. The solution, in the opinion of Roth, is in the introduction of tradable water rights and in letting the market govern the sector.[260]

In conclusion, it is noteworthy that a political approach to water issues is often limited to the extent that, even if the solutions proposed are potentially good, they often lack a multi-sector perspective. Indeed, such solutions are used to respond to sectorial concerns and therefore they represent the interests of the specific group that proposed them. Lastly, given that water is an object of public policy, the deficits in water governance have lowered citizens' confidence in the efficiency of the state to properly manage the service. It is also for this reason that the state should assign a central role to water policy-making in its agenda.

III *The Compromise and the IWRM Based on the River Basin Approach*

The idea of an IWRM[261] derives from the need to coordinate the different actors present in a specific river basin, because each of them may provide an important contribution to the system. Moreover, the exclusion of certain

---

258 Vergès, supra note 97, at 50.

259 G. Roth, *The Private Provision* of *Public Services in Developing Countries* (Oxford: Oxford University Press for the World Bank, 1987).

260 Jampaglia & Molinari, supra note 90, at 106–108.

261 For an exhaustive discussion of IWRM see A. T. Wolf (ed.), *Sharing Water, Sharing Benefits: Working Towards Effective Transboundary Water Resources Management* (Paris: UNESCO, 2010).

groups of stakeholders from the debate is at the origin of controversies whose settlement will cause a waste of resources.

It is strategic to gain information from all the actors from different sectors: the public, civil society, research centers, and the private sector. Only this interaction will achieve a deep knowledge and awarenes of the context in which water policies are inserted. The most appropriate level at which this exchange may occur is exactly the river basin, which should be regarded as the central unit of management.

In order to achieve good governance for the water system and a satisfactory quality of service, there is the need for financial resources, technical knowledge, and efficient organization.[262] However, neither the state nor civil society nor the private operators have enough resources and knowledge to reach this goal on their own: hence it is necessary for them to cooperate in planning their strategies and to act side-by-side.

IV *The Benefit of a Confrontation and Concurrence between Alternative Solutions*

The reflections presented throughout this monograph prove that neither a totally private solution nor sole public control resolve the common problems affecting water systems. Therefore, it is important to understand that only a flexible and open-to-discussion approach will overcome these challenges. In effect, as demonstrated throughout Part B, there are examples of efficient public water systems as well as successful cases of privatized ones, but the most advisable and flexibile water management solution resulted in being the public-private partnership. The decision-making process on water topics should not prioritize general objectives, like those of privatization, nationalization or decentralization, but more specific goals such as those associated with the integrated water management.[263]

Furthermore, the choice of conferring the system to a private or public operator should not be a definitive solution: the idea of a constant debate between alternative solutions and the concurrence between two or more options could benefit the sector. In effect, it avoids the inefficiencies generated by the permanence of the status quo granted by long-term contracts or by *de facto* monopolies. In this circumstance, the service provider, whether public

262 Fundación Chile, *Estándar Internacional de Gestión Sostenible del Agua* (Santiago de Chile, 2013).

263 Dourojeanni, supra note 91, 2014.

or private, is not incentivized to do its best and to improve its performance, because it knows it will maintain the position it has achieved.[264]

Nevertheless, it should be remembered that, even when the choice falls on a private provider, the state still has the ethical and practical obligation to guarantee that all citizens have access to water of a certain quality and quantity, because it is an essential good. Therefore, when the market is able to achieve a fair allocation of the resource, the state should just monitor it. On the contrary, when the market fails to equitably distribute water, the state has the irrevocable duty to intervene.[265] As Borzutzky said with regard to the Chilean case, 'the invisible hand of the free market genie (often requires) the very visible hand of the State to transform the existing economy and society'.[266] If the state does not comply with its obligations, likely because caring about water is not enough prioritized as it creates a less visible result than building infrastructures like a new highway, then the citizens themselves, through their political pressure, should urge governments to invest in the water system.[267]

It can be affirmed that, probably, the best water operators are those who have the humility to listen people's claims, the wisdom to stay informed on the surrounding social and environmental context, and the authority to implement the conscious decisions they have previously taken, in a dialogue with the civil society and other stakeholders.[268]

V *The Way Forward*

The three parts of this manuscript identify the flow from the RtW in the legal and abstract setting (predominantly in constitutions—Part A) to the right in context (i.e., water service models—Part B, and specifically the Chilean scenario—Part C). The linking bridging element is the discussion of the fundamental question on whether the right to water as a human right is in antithesis with privatization (Part A, Section IV). This question raises, across the manuscript, numerous other questions and possible answers. These reflections revolve around the role of the state, law, the private sector, the market,

264 Massarutto, supra note 90, at 105.

265 Alexander, supra note 32, at 21.

266 Ibid., at 31; S. Borzutzky, *Vital Connections: Politics, Social Security, and Inequality in Chile* (Notre Dame: Notre Dame University Press, 2002).

267 Sjölander Holland, supra note 6, at 164–165.

268 In the words of Dourojeanni: '*Probablemente los mejores gestores del agua son los que tienen la humildad de escuchar, la sapiencia para tomar decisiones informadas y la autoridad para aplicarlas*'. Dourojeanni, supra note 158, at 1.

and civil society in addressing the challenges presented by the implementation of the RtW. The following lessons can be sketched out, always bearing in mind that general conclusions can be difficult to formulate for specific water issues. However, common lessons from the Latin American experience for the global community dealing with water challenges can be identified. These lessons can be summarized as follows:

- In principle, the recognition of water as a human right in a constitution does not prevent the possibility of privatizing the service, as long as the state monitors the private provider's operations and complies with its obligations to ensure the RtW.
- The state's fulfilment of its duties towards its citizens with regards to the RtW are crucial to ensuring that, regardless whether there is privatization or public management of the water system, water is provided and managed as a human right.
- The public sector, civil society and the constitution (Part A) and the private sector and the market (Parts B and C) have key roles to play in the achievement of best practices in water governance in order to ensure multi-stakeholder compliance with the human right to water. Only the engagement of all the affected stakeholders in the debate on water will enable society to achieve a constructive and open-minded compromise for jointly facing today's water challenges.
- The frequent discrepancy between the law on the books and the law in action demonstrates that law is not always the best tool to resolve water issues. In this monograph, it is suggested that the legislators should be aware of this and plan legal strategies that are the closest possible to the needs of society. The balance between the norms proclaimed in theory and the law is presented as the goal for which water law-makers should aim.
- The role of the judicial branch in dealing with water issues is discussed with a view to underlining that, although courts should maintain a central position, it could be advisable to search for alternative way to settle disputes, such as arbitration, when it is possible and parties are willing to resort to such methods.
- There is an overall need for pragmatism in the debate on the RtW and water privatization. It is not possible to find the best water law only based on abstract statements. On the contrary, it is necessary to design good strategies to achieve an efficient water management for each river basin (the IWRM approach) with clear objectives (e.g. climate change mitigation and coastal management improvement).

At a more general level, the lessons water decision-makers and interested stakeholders can draw from this monograph can be summarized as follows:

- Transboundary, cross-sectorial, and multi-level cooperation is indispensable to properly addressing current water challenges.
- Any analysis of water systems' governance cannot investigate water law frameworks disconnected from its context, because it is the context that shapes and determines the final outcome of any water law and policy.
- The water debate should be considered as a strategic topic for LA countries given the risks for these states' stability if water conflicts emerge.
- The LA water policy-makers should look at the European context on water as the EU has been deeply influential in the debate on water privatization by developing new social rights (including the RtW indirectly), imposing certain environmental standards on national legislators, and developing principles for the creation of the common market and of fair competition among, *inter alia*, water services providers.
- The European legislators, in turn, should look at the lessons that LA cases, constitutions and jurisprudence can teach Europe as many Latin American countries have to face, on a broader scale than Europe, issues linked to severe drought, water shortages, water exploitation by multinationals, and water use conflicts.

List of References

Alexander, W. L., 'Enduring Contradictions of the Neoliberal State in Chile', *in* W. L. Alexander (ed.), *Lost in the Long Transition: Struggles for Social Justice in Neoliberal Chile*, pp. 1–33 (Lanham, MD: Lexington Books, 2009).

Americas Watch Committee, *Chile: Human Rights and the Plebiscite*, (New York: Americas Watch Committee, July 1988), http://www.corteidh.or.cr/tablas/4478.pdf.

Australia, State of Victoria, Department of Treasury and Finance, *Cost Recovery Guidelines* (2013).

Barbera, A., 'Commento all'art.2 della Costituzione', *in* G. Branca, *Commentario della Costituzione italiana* (Bologna: Zanichelli, 1975).

Barros, R., *Constitutionalism and Dictatorship Pinochet: the Junta, and the 1980 Constitution* (Cambridge: Cambridge University Press, 2002).

Bate, R., 'Let the Market Decide on Water Supply', *Mail & Guardian* (South Africa) (1 March 2001).

Bauer, C., 'Los Derechos de Agua y el Mercado: Efectos e implicancias del código de aguas chileno de 1981', *Revista de Derecho de Aguas* (IV & V) (1993).

Bobbio, N., *L'età dei diritti* (Torino: Einaudi, 1997).

Borzutzky, S., *Vital Connections: Politics, Social Security, and Inequality in Chile* (Notre Dame: Notre Dame University Press, 2002).

Brown, J., 'How Chile Might Leave the "Chilean Model" Behind: President Bachelet's Proposal to Reform the Country's Famously Laissez-Faire Water Laws', KBH Center for Energy, Law & Business, University of Texas at Austin, 3 July 2014. http://kbhenergycenter.utexas.edu/2014/07/03/how-chile-might-leave-the-chilean-model-behind-president-bachelets-proposal-to-reform-the-countrys-famously-laissez-faire-water-laws/.

Buchanan, J. M., 'Public Goods in Theory and Practice: A Note on the Minasian-Samuelson Discussion', *Journal of Law and Economics*, Vol. 10 (1967), pp. 193–197.

Chourabi, H., et al., 'Understanding Smart Cities: An Integrative Framework', in *Proceedings of the 45th Hawaii International Conference on System Sciences*, Maui, Hawaii, USA, 4–7 January 2012), pp. 2289–2297.

Consejo Andino de Ministros de Relaciones Exteriores, *Estrategia Andina para la Gestión Integrada de los Recursos Hídricos*, Decisión 763, vigésimo tercera Reunión Ordinaria del Consejo Andino de Ministros de Relaciones Exteriores, Lima, Peru, 22 August 2011.

Cordiero, J. L., *Constitutions Around the World: The View from Latin America, Institute of Developing Economies*, IDE Discussion Paper No. 164 (Chiba, Japan: Institute of Developing Economies, 2008).

Díaz, J., R. Lüders, & G. Wagner, *Economía Chilena 1810–2000. Producto Total y Sectorial. Una Nueva Mirada*, Documento de Trabajo IE-PUC No. 315 (Santiago: Pontificia Universidad Catolica de Chile, Instituto de Economia, 2007).

Donoso, F., & R. Fuster, *Crisis del agua: Diagnóstico y propuestas a partir de los consensos de la Iniciativa Agua y Medio Ambiente*, Andess Chile, Santiago de Chile, 24 July 2014.

Dourojeanni, A. C., & A. Jouravlev, *El Código de Aguas de Chile: Entre la ideología y la realidad*, (Santiago de Chile: CEPAL, 1999).

Dourojeanni, A. C., *Gestión integrada por Cuencas: una elección politica de gobernanza sobre territorios delimitados por razones naturales* (Quito: Fundación Chile, 2010).

Dourojeanni, A. C., *La Gestión del Agua en los Límites de Disponibilidad en Latinoamérica* (Santiago: Gerencia de Agua & Medio Ambiente, Fundación Chile, 2012a).

Dourojeanni, A. C., *Thematic Study on the Common Problems and Challenges in the Integrated Management of Water Resources and Coasts in the Context of Climate Change in Latin America*, EuropeAid/129783/C/SER/multi, Specific contract No. 2012/298550, Version 1 (2012b).

Dourojeanni, A. C., *Los retos que impone la gestión del agua a la sustentabilidad empresarial*, Documento de divulgación de Acción RSE (Santiago de Chile: Fundación Chile, 2014a).

Dourojeanni, A. C., *Reformas a las leyes de agua en América Latina* (Santiago de Chile; Fundación Chile, 2014b).

Dourojeanni, A. C., & C. Galleguillos, *SuizAgua Andina Chile: RSEAgua, un compromiso necesario para la Sustenabilidad* (Santiago de Chile: Fundación Chile, 2014).

European Commission, Directorate-General Regional Policy, *Guidelines for Successful Public-Private Partnerships* (March 2003), http://ec.europa.eu/regional_policy/sources/docgener/guides/ppp_en.pdf.

European Commission, Communication from the Commission on the European Citizens' Initiative 'Water and sanitation are a human right! Water is a public good, not a commodity!', COM(2014) 177 final, 19 March 2014.

European Communities, Charter of Fundamental Rights of the European Union, 2012/C 326/02 (26 October 2012).

Eustace, R., 'Fluid Constitutions: A Latin American Phenomenon Council on Hemispheric Affairs', Council on Hemispheric Affairs (3 July 2014), http://www.coha.org/fluid-constitutions-a-latin-american-phenomenon/comment-page-1/.

Finnegan, W., 'Letter from Bolivia—Leasing the Rain', *The New Yorker*, (8 April 2002) at 43.

Franco, H. J., & L. Armella, *La cuenca Matanza-RiachueLo: Estado de situación de La sentencia de La Corte Suprema de Justicia de La nación en Los autos "Mendoza, Beatriz y otros c/ Estado Nacional"*, Instituto de Política Ambiental (2010).

Fundación Chile, *Estándar Internacional de Gestión Sostenible del Agua* (Santiago de Chile, April 2013).

Ginsburg, T., *The Lifespan of Written Constitutions* (Chicago: University of Illinois, College of Law, 2007).

Hachfeld, D., P. Terhorst, & O. Hoedeman, *Progressive Public Water Management in Europe. In Search of Exemplary Cases* (The Transnational Institute and Corporate Europe Observatory, 2009).

Hearne, R. R., & G. Donoso, 'Water Institutional Reforms in Chile', *Water Policy* Vol. 7 (2005), pp. 53–69.

Jamieson, J., *PPP in Water and Sanitation: Don't Believe the Hype* (International Finance Corporation, 2010).

Jampaglia, B., & E. Molinari, *Salvare l'Acqua* (Milan: Feltrinelli Editore, 2010).

Justo, J. B., *El derecho humano al agua y al saneamiento frente a los Objetivos de Desarrollo del Milenio* (Santiago de Chile: CEPAL, 2013). Kleemeier, E. & H. Lockwood, *Public-Private Partnerships for Rural Water Service*, Briefing Note No. 4 (The Hague: IRC International Water and Sanitation Centre, 2012).

Kornfeld, I. E., 'Water: A Public Good or a Commodity?', *in Proceedings of the Annual Meeting of the American Society of International Law, Confronting Complexity*, Vol. 106 (Cambridge: Cambridge University Press, 2012), pp. 49–52.

Laserre, F., *Acqua. Spartizione di una risorsa* (Milan: Ponte alle Grazie srl, 2004).

Lee, T. R., & A. Jouravlev, *Prices, Property and Market in Water Allocation* (Santiago de Chile: CEPAL, 1998).

Levitsky, S., & M. V. Murillo, *Building Institutions on Weak Foundations: Lessons from Latin America* (Harvard University and Columbia University, 2012).

Loveman, B., *Chile: The Legacy of Hispanic Capitalism* (Oxford: Oxford Universiy Press, 2001).

Lüders, R., *La Misión Klein-Saks, los Chicago Boys y la Política Económica*, Documento de Trabajo IE-PUC, No. 411 (Santiago: Pontificia Universidad Catolica de Chile, Instituto de Economia, 2012).

Marin, P., *Public-Private Partnerships for Urban Water Utilities: A Review of Experiences in Developing Countries* (Washington, D.C.: The World Bank, 2009).

Massarutto, A., *Privati dell'acqua?* (Bologna: Il Mulino 2011).

McGraw, G., 'Defining and Defending the Right to Water and its Minimum Core: Legal Construction and the Role of National Jurisprudence,' *Loyola University Chicago International Law Review*, Vol. 8(2) (2011), pp. 127–204.

Mohajeri, S., B. Knothe, D-N. Lamothe & J-A. Faby (eds.), *European Water Management between Regulation and Competition* (Luxembourg: Office for Official Publicatons of the European Communities, 2003).

Navia, P., & J. Rios-Figueroa, 'The Constitutional Adjudication Mosaic of Latin America', *Comparative Political Studies*, Vol. 38 (2005), pp. 189–217.

Negretto, G., 'The Durability of Constitutions in Changing Environments: A Study on Constitutional Stability in Latin America', paper presented at the American Political Science Association Meeting, Philadelphia, USA, 31 August 2006.

Negretto, G., *The Durability of Constitutions in Changing Environments: Explaining Constitutional Replacement in Latin America*, Working Paper No. 350 (South Bend, IN: University of Notre Dame, Helen Kellogg Institute for International Studies, 2008).

Negretto, G., *Replacing and Amending Constitutions: The Logic of Constitutional Change in Latin America*, paper prepared for delivery at the American Political Science Association Meeting, Washington, D.C., USA, 1–4 September 2011.

North, D., *Institutions, Institutional Change and Economic Performance* (Cambridge: Cambridge University Press, 2004).

Organisation for Economic Co-operation and Development (OECD), *Key Messages and Draft Principles on Stakeholder Engagement*, Draft for Working Group Consultation, 18 April 2014, in preparation for the 3rd Meeting of the OECD Water Governance Initiative, 28–29 April 2014, Madrid, Spain.

Ostrom, E., *Governing the Commons: The Evolution of Institutions for Collective Action* (Cambridge: Cambridge University Press, 1990).

Parena, R., & E. Smeets, 'Benchmarking Initiatives in the Water Industry', *Water Science and Technology*, Vol. 44 (2–3) (2001), pp. 103–110.

Portuguez, J. M., & V. Dubois Cisneros, *Implementación del derecho humano al agua en América Latina, Proceso Regional de las Américas Sub-región América del Sur, VII Foro Mundial del Agua, Corea* (Caracas: Corporación Andina de Fomento, 2015).

Ringskog, K., M. E. Hammond, & A. Locussol, *Using Management and Lease-Affermage Contracts for Water Supply. How Effective are They in Improving Service Delivery?*, World Bank Grid Lines No.12 (Washington, D.C.: Public-Private Advisory Facility, The World Bank, 2006).

Rogers, P., & A. W. Hall, *Effective Water Governance*, Global Water Partnership Technical Committee, Background Paper no.7 (Stockholm: Global Water Partnership, 2003).

Roth, G., *The Private Provision of Public Services in Developing Countries* (Oxford: Oxford University Press for the World Bank, 1987).

Rulli, M., & J. B. Justo, *Guía de derechos humanos para empresas: proteger, respetar y remediar: todos ganamos* (Buenos Aires: Programa de las Naciones Unidas para el Desarrollo, Red Argentina Pacto Global, 2012).

Sáez-Muñoz, C. R., '*Privatized Water Rights and Services in Chile 1981–2011: Flowing Towards the Mainstream?*' (Ph.D. Thesis No. 1035, Graduate Institute, Geneva, 2014).

Salman, M. A. S., & S. McInerney-Lankford, *The Human Right to Water: Legal and Policy Dimensions* (Washington, D.C.: The World Bank, 2004).

Salman, M. A. S., 'The Future of International Water Law: Regional Approaches to Shared Watercourses?', *in* M. S. Arsanjani et al. (eds), *Looking to the Future: Essays on International Law in Honor of W. Michael Reisman* (The Hague: Martinus Nijhoff Publishers, 2010), pp. 907–928.

Salman, M. A. S., 'The Human Right to Water—Challenges of Implementation', *in Proceedings of the Annual Meeting of the American Society of International Law, Confronting Complexity*, Vol. 106 (Cambridge: Cambridge University Press, 2012), pp. 44–46.

Salman, M. A. S., 'The Human Right to Water and Sanitation: Is the Obligation Deliverable?', *Water International* (2014) doi: 10.1080/02508060.2015.986616.

Schuch de Azambuja, L., et al., 'A Smart City Initiative: A Case Study of Porto Alegre', *in Proceedings of the 15th Annual International Conference on Digital Government Research*, Aguascalientes, Mexico, 18–21 June 2014, pp. 245–252.

Schulte, P., *Corporate Water Disclosure Guidelines. Toward a Common Approach to Reporting Water Issues* (Oakland, CA: The Pacific Institute, The CEO Water Mandate, 2014).

Segerfeldt, F., *Acqua in vendita?* (2003), trad.it. (Torino: IBL, 2011).

Sjölander Holland, A-C., *Il Business dell'Acqua* (2005), trad.it, (Milan: Editorale Jaka Book SpA, 2006).

Staiano, S., 'Note sul diritto fondamentale all'acqua. Proprietà del bene, gestione del servizio, ideologie della privatizzazione', *Federalismi.it*, Vol. 5 (2011).

Szigeti Correa, C., *Reformas Constitucionales en materia de agua y reformas al Código de Aguas*, Comisiones de Trabajo, Proyectos de Ley y Mociones Parlamentarias presentadas a tramitación (1992 y 2012) (Santiago de Chile: Edición Sara Larraín, Programa Chile Sustentable, 2013).

Tan, V., *The Public-Private Partnership* (PPP) (London: Advocates for International Development, 2012).

Tega, D., *I diritti in crisi. Tra Corti nazionali e Corte europea di Strasburgo* (Milan: Università degli Studi di Milano Bicocca, 2012).

United Nations, *International Covenant on Economic, Social and Cultural Rights*, UN General Assembly Res. 2200A (XXI), 16 December 1966.

Vergès, J-F., *Experiencias relevantes de marcos institucionales y contratos en agua potable y alcantarillado* (Santiago de Chile: CEPAL, 2010).

Winpenny, J., *Financing Water for All*, Report of the World Panel on Financing Water Infrastructure, Chair, Michel Camdessus (World Water Council, 3rd World Water Forum and Global Water Partnership, March 2003), http://www.worldwatercouncil.org/en/publications/financing-water-all.

Wolf, A.T. (ed.), *Sharing Water, Sharing Benefits: Working Towards Effective Transboundary Water Resources Management* (Paris: UNESCO, 2010).

World Health Organization (WHO), *Guidelines for Drinking-water Quality* (Geneva: WHO, 2011).

Zañartu Rosselot, H., 'Aguas subterráneas: ¿Necesidad de un nuevo enfoque?', *Revista de Derecho Administrativo Económico de Recursos Naturales*, Vol. 3(2) (2001), pp. 539–545.

Zolo, D., 'Nuovi diritti e globalizzazione', *Treccani.it L'Enciclopedia Italiana* (2009), http://www.treccani.it/enciclopedia/nuovi-diritti-e-globalizzazione_%28XXI-Secolo%29/.

Chilean Laws

Constitución Política De La República De Chile, Decreto Supremo 1.150, Ministerio Secretaría General de la Presidencia, 1980.

Régimen de los Servicios Públicos Domiciliarios, Ley n.142, 11 July 1994.

Ley Indigena 19.253, 5 de Octubre de 1993.

Código de Aguas, 13 de Agosto de 1981, D.F.L. Nº 1.122.

Boletín N. 7543–12, Comparado Proyecto de Ley que reforma el Código de Aguas.

Ley General de Servicios de Saneamiento n. 26338, 24 July 1994.

Lei Nº 54/2005. DR 219 SÉRIE I-A de 2005-11-15. Estabelece a titularidade dos recursos hídricos.

Reforma del Código de Aguas, Ley Nº 20.017, 11 de Mayo de 2005.

Ley Nº 19.300, sobre Bases Generales del Medio Ambiente, 9 de Marcio de 1994.

D.F.L. Nº 850/1997 and D.F.L. Nº 1.115/1969 del Ministerio de Obras Públicas.

EU Law

Charter of Fundamental Rights of the European Union, 2000/C 364/01.

European Communities, Council Directive 1998/83/EC of 3 November 1998 on the quality of water intended for human consumption, OJ L 330, 5 December 1998.

European Communities, Directive 2000/60/EC of the European Parliament and of the Council of 23 October 2000 establishing a framework for Community action in the field of water policy, OJ L 327, 22 December 2000, as amended by Decision 2455/2001/EC, Directive 2008/32/EC and Directive 2009/31/EC.

European Communities, Consolidated Version of Treaty on the Functioning of the European Union, 2008 OJ C 115/47.

Case Law

Corte Constitucional de Colombia, Sentencias T-539/ 1993, T-1104/2005, T-091/ 2010, T-381/2009, T-418/2010, T-143/2010, T-595/ 2002, T-418/2010, T-614/2010, T-717/2010, T-740/2011, T-641/15, T-139/16, T-131/16, and T-100/17. Texts available at http://www.corteconstitucional.gov.co/relatoria/.

Sentencia M.1569.XL/2006, MENDOZA Beatriz Silvia y Otros C/ ESTADO NACIONAL y Otros S/ Daños y Perjuicios (daños derivados de la contaminación ambiental del Río Matanza-Riachuelo). Available at http://www.elaw.org/system/files/caso.mendoza.riachuelo.pdf.

Cámara de Apelaciones en lo Contencioso Administrativo y Tributario de la Ciudad de Buenos Aires, Causa Nº 20898/0, Asociación Civil por la Igualdad y la Justicia c/ GCBA s/ amparo, 18.07.2007.

Corte Constitucional de Perù, Sentencia n.6546/2006. Available at http://www.tc.gob.pe/jurisprudencia/2007/06546-2006-AA.html.

Corte Constitucional de Bolivia, Sentencia 684/2010-R, 19 July 2010.

Corte Constitucional de Bolivia, Sentencia 1106/2010-R, 27 August 2010.

Corte Constitucional de Bolivia, Sentencia 1230/2016-S3, 8 November 2011.

Corte Constitucional de México, Sentencia 49/2014.

www.ingramcontent.com/pod-product-compliance
Lightning Source LLC
Chambersburg PA
CBHW031330230926
51848CB00001B/165
* 9 7 8 9 0 0 4 3 6 7 8 0 7 *